Street by Street

STRATF ORD UPON-AVON
ROYAL LEAMINGTON SPA, WARWICK
Alveston, Cubbington, Haseley, Radford Semele, Shottery, Tiddington, Wellesbourne, Wilmcote

1st edition May 2001

© Automobile Association Developments Limited 2001

This product includes map data licensed from Ordnance Survey® with the permission of the Controller of Her Majesty's Stationery Office. © Crown copyright 2000. All rights reserved. Licence No: 399221.

Published by AA Publishing (a trading name of Automobile Association Developments Limited, whose registered office is Norfolk House, Priestley Road, Basingstoke, Hampshire, RG24 9NY. Registered number 1878835).

Mapping produced by the Cartographic Department of The Automobile Association.

A CIP Catalogue record for this book is available from the British Library.

Printed by GRAFIASA S.A., Porto, Portugal

The contents of this atlas are believed to be correct at the time of the latest revision. However, the publishers cannot be held responsible for loss occasioned to any person acting or refraining from action as a result of any material in this atlas, nor for any errors, omissions or changes in such material. The publishers would welcome information to correct any errors or omissions and to keep this atlas up to date. Please write to Publishing, The Automobile Association, Fanum House, Basing View, Basingstoke, Hampshire, RG21 4EA.

Ref: ML112

Key to map pages — ii-iii

Key to map symbols — iv-1

Enlarged scale pages — 2-7

Street by Street — 8-35

Index – towns & villages — 36

Index – streets — 37-41

Index – featured places — 41-42

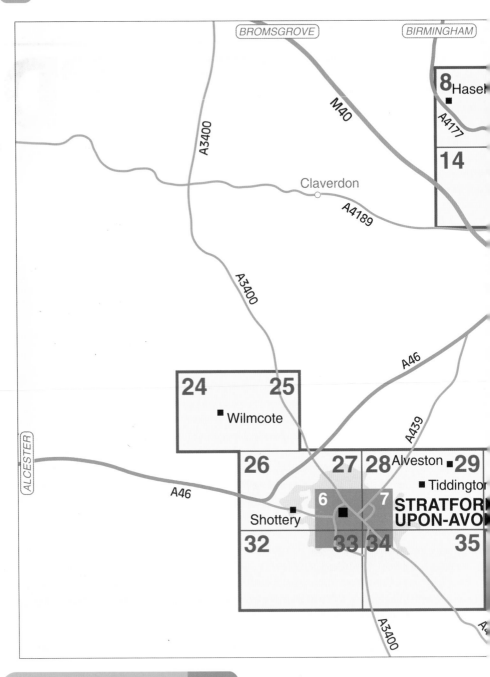

BROMSGROVE   BIRMINGHAM

8 Hase

A4177

M40

A3400

14

Claverdon

A4189

A3400

A46

24   **25**

■ Wilmcote

A439

ALCESTER

26   **27**   **28** Alveston ■ **29**

■ Tiddington

A46

6   **7** **STRATFOR**
Shottery ■   ■   **UPON-AVO**

32   **33** **34**   **35**

A3400

Enlarged scale pages 1:10,000 6.3 inches to 1 mile

0   1/4   miles   1/2

0   1/4   1/2   kilometres   3/4   1

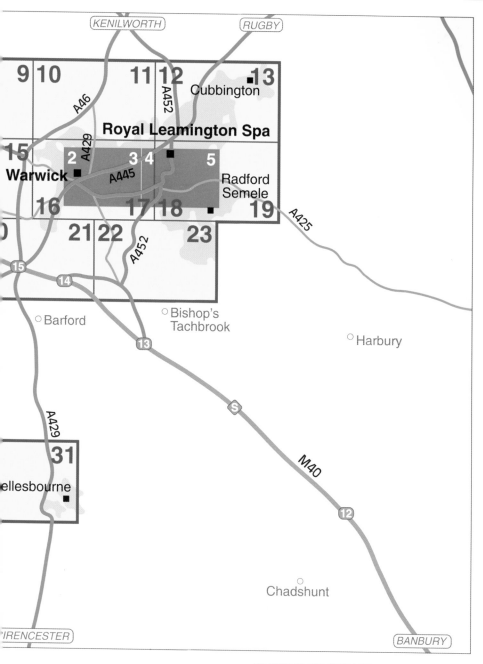

KENILWORTH   RUGBY

9 10   11 12 Cubbington 13

A46

A452

A429

Royal Leamington Spa

15   2 3 4 5

Warwick   A445   Radford
Semele

16   17 18   19

A425

21 22   23

A452

15

14

Barford   Bishop's
Tachbrook

13   Harbury

A429

31   S

ellesbourne   M40

12

Chadshunt

CIRENCESTER   BANBURY

4.2 inches to 1 mile   **Scale of main map pages** 1:15,000

0   1/4   miles   1/2   3/4   1

0   1/4   1/2   kilometres 3/4   1   1 1/4   1 1/2

iv

Junction 9 Motorway & junction

Services Motorway service area

Primary road single/dual carriageway

Services Primary road service area

A road single/dual carriageway

B road single/dual carriageway

Other road single/dual carriageway

Restricted road

Private road

One way street

Pedestrian street

Track/ footpath

Road under construction

Road tunnel

P Parking

P+ Park & Ride

Bus/Coach station

Railway & main railway station

Railway & minor railway station

Underground station

Light Railway & station

Preserved private railway

LC Level crossing

Tramway

Ferry route

Airport runway

Boundaries- borough/ district

Mounds

93 Page continuation 1:15,000

7 Page continuation to enlarged scale 1:10,000

River/canal, lake, pier

Aqueduct, lock, weir

465
▲
Winter Hill
Peak (with height in metres)

Beach

Coniferous woodland

Broadleaved woodland

Mixed woodland

Park

Cemetery

Built-up area

Featured building

City wall

A&E Accident & Emergency hospital

Toilet

Toilet with disabled facilities

Petrol station

PH Public house

PO Post Office

Public library

ℹ Tourist Information Centre

Castle

Historic house/ building

Wakehurst Place NT National Trust property

M Museum/ art gallery

† Church/chapel

Country park

Theatre/ performing arts

Cinema

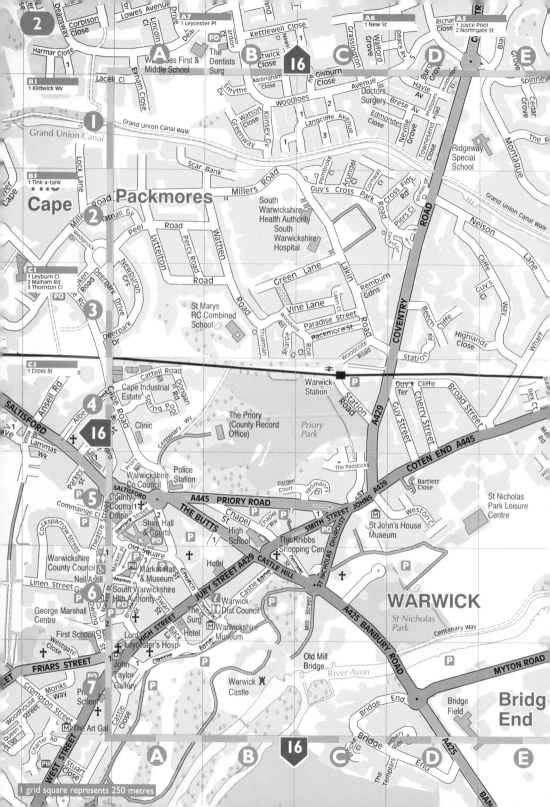

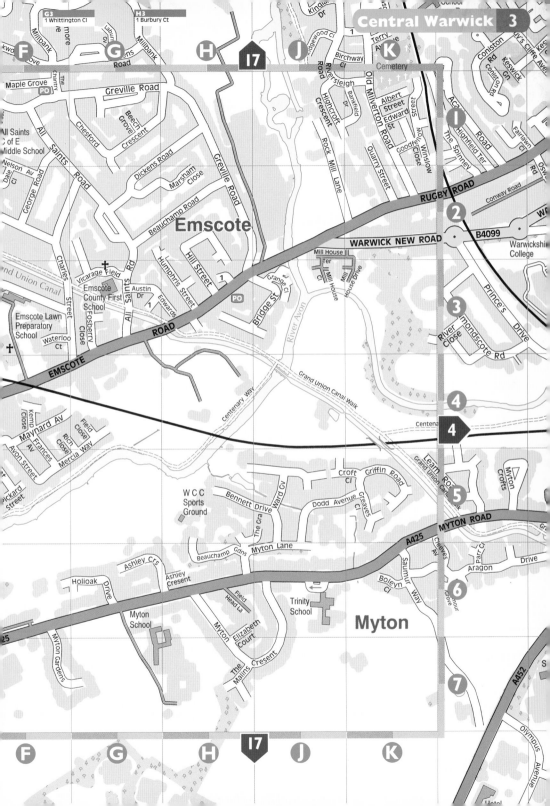

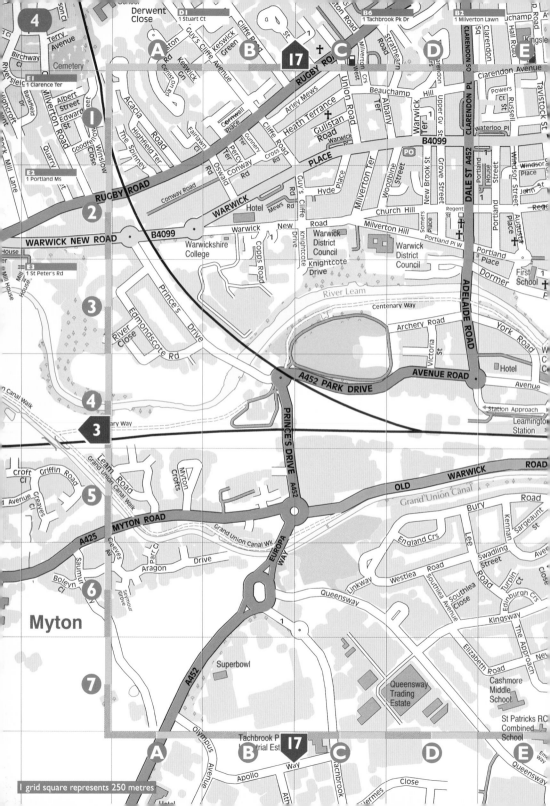

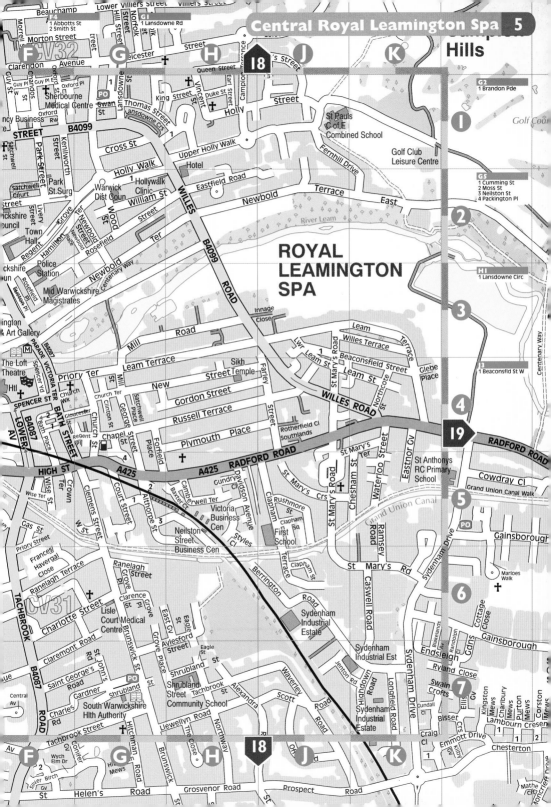

Hills

ROYAL
LEAMINGTON
SPA

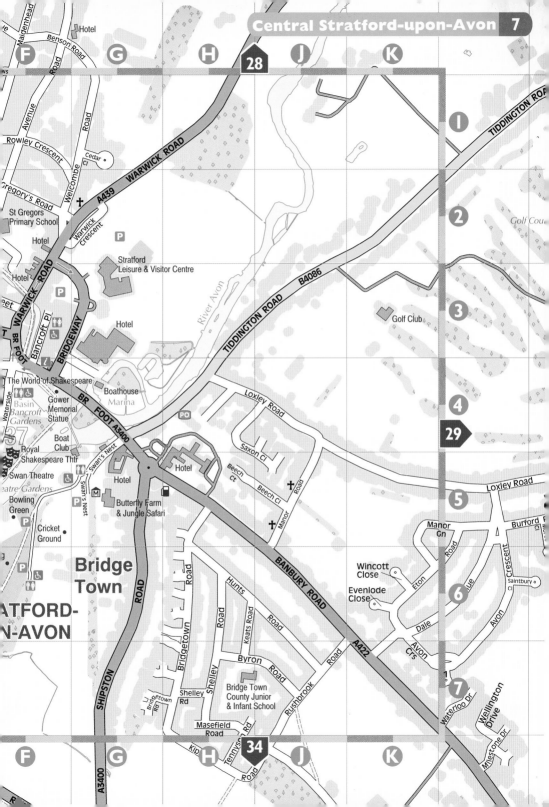

F G H J K

28

Maldenhead

Hotel

Benson Road

Rowley Crescent

Cedar Cl

Welcombe

WARWICK ROAD

A439

Avenue

Gregory's Road

St Gregors Primary School

Warwick Crescent

P

Hotel

Stratford Leisure & Visitor Centre

Hotel

WARWICK ROAD

BRIDGEWAY

P

Bancroft Pl

BR FOOT

Hotel

River Avon

TIDDINGTON ROAD

B4086

TIDDINGTON ROAD

Golf Course

Golf Club

The World of Shakespeare

Waterside

Basin

Bancroft Gardens

Gower Memorial Statue

Boathouse Marina

BR FOOT A3400

PO

Loxley Road

Royal Shakespeare Thtr

Boat Club

Swan's Nest

Swan Theatre

Theatre Gardens

Bowling Green

Swan's Nest

M

Hotel

Hotel

Butterfly Farm & Jungle Safari

Saxon Cl

Beech Ct

Beech Cl

Manor Road

Road

Loxley Road

29

P

Cricket Ground

Bridge Town

P

STRATFORD-
ON-AVON

SHIPSTON ROAD

A3400

Bridgetown Road

Hunts Road

Keats Road

Shelley Road

Byron Road

BANBURY ROAD

Road

Rushbrook Road

A422

Manor Gn

Eton Road

Avenue

Burford

Crescent

Saintbury Cl

Avon

Wincott Close

Evenlode Close

Dale

Avon Crs

Bridgetown Rd

Shelley Rd

Bridge Town County Junior & Infant School

Masefield Road

Tennyson Rd

Kip

34

Waterloo Dr

Wellington Drive

Milestone Dr

F G H J K

Waste Green
A3
1 The Green

8
BIRMINGHAM ROAD

D5
1 Ilmington Cl
2 Winderton Av

A   B   C   D

I

2

Old Manor
Farm

Haseley
Business
Centre

Haseley
Manor

3
Stoney Lane

BIRMINGHAM ROAD

Haseley

Kites Nest

Beausale Lane

1

The Ferncumbe
C of E Community
Primary School

A4177

Home
Farm

4

B4439

Hatton

Welford
CV

Beausale Lane

Armsc

Hatton
House

Canal Rd

1

2

5
Grand Union Canal

Grand Union Canal Walk

Grand Union Canal Walk

Grand Union Canal Walk

Middle Lock
Lane

A   B   ▼ I4   C   D

Hatton
● Country World

I grid square represents 500 metres

E5
1 Alderminster Gv
2 Rowborough Cl
3 Tidmington Cl

E
F
Bulloak Farm
G
H
Good
Farm

Deer Park
Farm

I

Kingstanding
Farm

Larch
Covert

2

3

Prospect
Farm

10

Turkey
Farm

4

Dorsington
Close

Barcheston Drive

Charingworth Drive

Combroke
Gv

Ebrington

Drive

1 2

3

5

Wedgnock
Park Farm

E
A4177
BIRMINGHAM
F
15
G
H

WARWICK BY-PASS

D5
1 Congreve Cl
2 Cooke Cl
3 Dennett Cl
4 Sheldon Gv
5 Weale Gv

C5
1 Berwick Cl
2 Drayton Ct
3 Hicks Cl
4 Linden Cl
5 Moore Cl

Woodcote

A   B   C   D

Woodcote Drive

Home Farm

Lane

Waller Cl

Quarry Flds

PO

Wootton Court

1

Larch Covert

2

Gaveston Cross

3

Prospect Fm

9

Centenary Way

4

Warwick By-Pass

Woodloes Farm

Woodloes Lane

Guy's Cliffe

5

Woodloes Lane

A46(T)

Wedgnock Lane

Welton Road

Rothwell Road

A   B   C   D

Primrose Hill

Ridgeley Cl
Wise Gv
Welsh
Wade Gv
Drive
Hathaway
Eborall Close
Hughes Close
Norton Dr
Lee Cl
Kites
Inchford Av
Westcliff Dr
Woodloes Av
Cowper Ct
Yardley
North
Hind
Kirby Avenue
Primrose Hill

16

Crane
Crane Av
Corbison Close
Hawes Av
Knoll Dr
Kettlewell Close
Grassington Av
Walford Grove
Harmar C
Deansway
Austwick Close
Gisburn Close
Hebden Av
South
Lacell Close
Middle School
The Dentists Surg
Woodloes
Avenue
Doctors Surg

Woodloes Park

1 grid square represents 500 metres

G5
1 Ravensdale Av
2 St Albans Cl

H5
1 Colbourne Gv Dr

E **F** **G** **H**

Wootton
E First
chool

The Ha
Croft
Road

arsh Road

ll Wootton Road

**Leek
Wootton**

Hill Wootton Road

KENILWORTH

Old Le
Rugby

**Hill
Wootton**

I

River Avon

A46(T)

B4115

ll Saints C of E
(VA) Community
Primary School

2

Warwick
Nuffield
Hospital

Old Milve

3

12

Sandy Lane

**Old
Milverton**

†

Old Milverton Road

4

A429

River Avon

†

Range
Meadow
Cl

Hopton Crofts

Overell Gv

Lamintone Dr

Milverton

Fairhurst Dr

Loveday
Cl

Fryer Av

Davis
Cl

1

Avonlea
Eaton
Cl

1

Kendal
Av

Penrith
Cl

Borrowdale Dr

Ennerdale

Cockermouth

Rydale Cl

Close

Windermere Dr

Mose

The

Astley
Cl

5

The Fairways

Troutbeck
Av

Wasdale

Trinity RC
School

Ullswater

Beverley Road

Freemans Cl

Gaveston
Rd

Greatheed R

wheathill Cl

4

E 1 **F** **G** **H**

ow
Rd
Lilac Gv

5

Oakwood Grove

6

Laburnum
Grove

PattensRoad

Millbank

St James
Meadow Rd

King Edward Rd

Ridgewood
Close

Cliffe

Old Milverton Road

Guy's

17

2

1

Terry
Av

Cem

Brookhurst
Primary
School

2

Coniston
Road

Keswick
Green

Cliffe Road

St Mark's
Road

H

3

Union

Beauch

Strathearn

Cedar

spinney

Maple
Gv

PO

3

Greville

High
Crs

Bankfield

Albert
St

Conway Rd

St Mark's Rd

Conrley Ms

2

ROAD

LEICESTER

B445

E   F   G   H

RUGBY ROAD

I

G1
1 Willow Shts Mdw

South
Cubbington
Wood

cotton Mi
Thorn Stile
Close
Spinney
Three
Cornered
Close

Cubbington

Broadway

Windmill Hill

Stonehouse Close

Boddington Close

Ledbrook Road

Church Lane

Church Hi

Cubbington C of E
Combined School

2

G2
1 Chamberlain Cl

Kenilworth Road

Balmoral Way

Beaufort Avenue

Girvan Grove

Dunblane Drive

West View Road

High View Rd

South View Road

Our Lady &
St Teresas RC
Combined School

Queen St

High Street

Hill Crescent

Ladycroft

North Brookfield Rd

Knightley

Penns

Price Rd

Cross Lane

New Street

Mill

Lane

PO

B4453 Road

Hill Farm

Leighton Close

Oakridge Rd

Meadow Cl

Parklands Avenue

Sherwood Wk

Epsom

Valley

Kempton Crs

Ascot Ride

Aintree Drive

Epping Way

Delamere Way

Wye Close

Severn Cl

Elan Close

Langdale Close

Charnwood Way

Fell GV

Crickli Wa

Newland Rd

The Gle

Lillington

New Manor
Farm

Offchurch

3

Lowe
Gran

Glebe
Farm

Road

4

Welsh Road

Mason Avenue

Sudbury Cl

Denby Cl

Clare Close

Bunbury

Compton Close

itton Road

Lane

Ford
Farm

5

Har
Far

**Campion
Hills**

E   F   **19**   G   H

14

Grand Union Canal

Grand Union Canal Walk

Grand Union Canal Walk

Union Canal Walk

Middle Lock Lane

A **B** **8** **C** **D**

I

Hatton Country World

Budbrooke Farm

Nunhold Farm
Nunhold Business Centre

2

M40

3

Norton

Grove Park

4

Curlieu

Whitehill Wood

Grove Park

5

Lane

Warboro Farm

M40

HENLEY ROAD A4189 HENLEY

A Low B Norton **C** **D**

1 grid square represents 500 metres

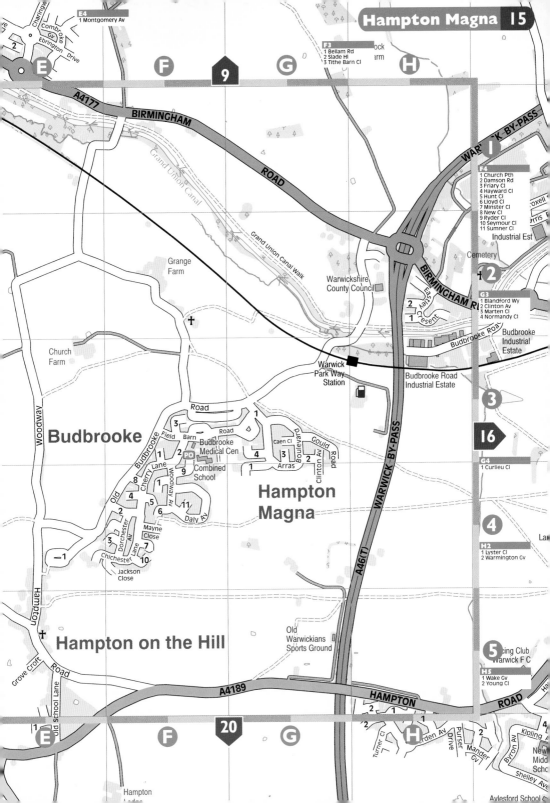

E4
1 Montgomery Av

F3
1 Bellam Rd
2 Slade Hl
3 Tithe Barn Cl

F4
1 Church Pth
2 Damson Rd
3 Friary Cl
4 Hayward Cl
5 Hunt Cl
6 Lloyd Cl
7 Minster Cl
8 New Cl
9 Ryder Cl
10 Seymour Cl
11 Sumner Cl

Industrial Est

Cemetery

C3
1 Blandford Wy
2 Clinton Av
3 Marten Cl
4 Normandy Cl

Budbrooke
Industrial
Estate

Budbrooke Road
Industrial Estate

G4
1 Curlieu Cl

H2
1 Lyster Cl
2 Warmington Gv

H5
1 Wake Gv
2 Young Cl

A4177

BIRMINGHAM ROAD

Grand Union Canal

Grand Union Canal Walk

Grange
Farm

Warwickshire
County Council

Church
Farm

WARWICK BY-PASS

BIRMINGHAM RD

East Kayte Crescent

Warwick
Park Way
Station

Budbrooke Road

Woodway

Budbrooke

Road

Field

Barn

Road

Budbrooke
Medical Cen

Caen Cl

Arras

Engleme

Gould Road

Clinton Av

PO

Combined
School

Cherry Lane

Old

Woodway Av

Daly Av

Mayne
Close

Dorchester Av

Lane

Chichester

Jackson
Close

**Hampton
Magna**

Hampton

A46(T)

WARWICK BY-PASS

Old
Warwickians
Sports Ground

†

Hampton on the Hill

Grove Croft

Road

Old School Lane

A4189

HAMPTON ROAD

cing Club
Warwick F C

Turner Cl

arden Av

Purser

Drive

Mander
Gv

Byron Av

Kipling

New
Midd
Sch

Shelley Av

Hampton
Lodge

Aylesford School

E1
1 Almond Gv
2 Arden Cl
3 The Chantry
4 Larch Gv
5 Millbank
6 Sycamore Gv

E2
1 Dale Cl
2 Guy's Cl
3 Highlands Cl
4 Nelson Av

E3
1 Basant Cl
2 Ilex Ct
3 Kemp Cl
4 Meadow Rd
5 Rich Cl

F1
1 Beech Gv

F2
1 A Edwards Dr
2 Burbury Ct
3 Chesford Crs
4 Fosberry Cl
5 Whittington Cl

F3
1 Field Cl
2 The Grange
3 Ward Gv

G1
1 Birchway Cl
2 Blandford Rd
3 Edward St

H1
1 Cross Rd
2 Derwent Cl

H2
1 Mews Rd
2 Milverton Lawn

H4
1 Cleeves Av
2 Seymour Gv

Trinity RC School

Brookhurst Primary School

All Saints C of E Middle School

Emscote

Emscote Lawn Preparatory School

First School

Myton

Warwickshire College

Warwick New Road

WARWICK

W C C Sports Ground

Nicholas Park Leisure Centre

Myton School

Trinity School

Bridge End

Heathcote Hill Farm

Tachbrook Park Industrial Est

Queens Trading Estate

Superbowl

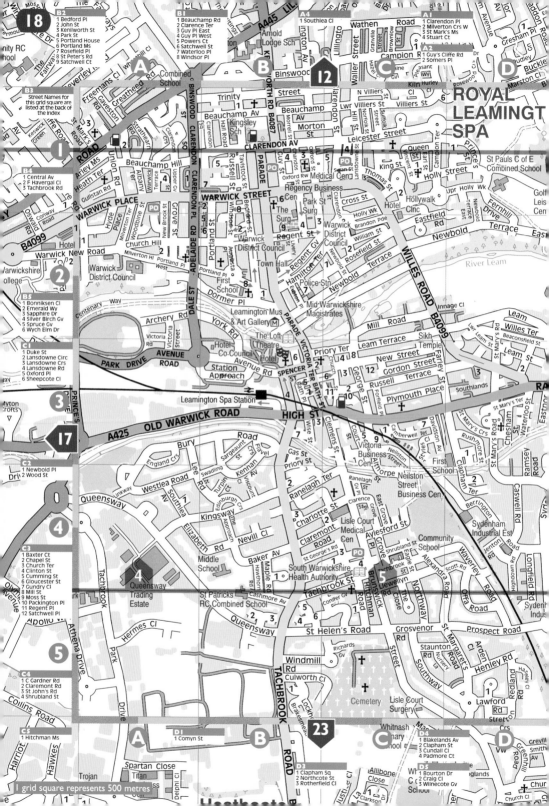

E3
1 Fellmore Gv

E
F
13
G
H

I

E4
1 Barton Crs
2 Burford Ms
3 Coningsby Cl
4 Newbury Cl
5 Randolph Cl
6 Standlake Ms
7 Waverton Ms
8 Weston Cl

2

E5
1 Blenheim Crs
2 Hidcote Cl
3 Kilby Gv

F4
1 Chatsworth Gdns
2 Grenfell Cl
3 Radbrook Wy
4 Springwell Rd
5 Wentworth Rd

3

F5
1 Baddesley Cl

Campion Hills

Golf Course

Newbold Comyn Park

Redhouse Farm

River Leam

Centenary Wy

Cowdray Cl
ROAD
A425
Gainsborough
Marloes Walk
Ledbury Road
Cottage Close
Kingston Ms
Charlbury Ms
Purton Ms
Corston Ms
Alderton Ms
Lambourn Crs
Middle School
Drive
Portway Cl
Vermont Gv
Stidfall Gv
Marcroft Place
Pennystone
Chatsworth Gv
Beaulieu Pk
Gulliman's Wy

Grand Union Canal Walk
Grand Union Canal

4

G5
1 Hemmings Cl

Woburn
Marlborough Dr
Calder Wk
Longleat
Pack Wood
Croft
Medical Centre
Charlecote Gdns
Mathe Cft
Bank Cft
Newdigate
Cobden Av
Coughton Dr

Danebury Crs
Eanton Rd

Radford Semele C of E Combined
The Gardens
Hamilton Rd
Meadow
Chapman Close
Slade

Church End
Kinghurst
School Lane
Spring La
Semele Close
Hatherell Rd
Hallfields
Lay Gdns
Lythall Rd
PO
Thornley Cl

Offchurch Lane
The Creswoldes
Chance Flds

5

H5
1 Overtons Cl

Sydenham
Campion School

Radford Semele

Godfrey Cl
Lewis
St Nicholas
Williams Rd
Valley Rd
The Valley
Road

E
F
CV31
G
H

Cricket

E1
1 Longfellow Av
2 Robins Gv
3 Shakespeare Av
4 Tennyson Av

F1
1 Alders Gv
2 Fisher's Ct
3 Stratford Rd

Cricket

Racing Club
Warwick F C

Warwick Sports Club

Hampton

Burns Av

Browning Av

Noble

Temple Grove

Wordsworth Av

E

F

G

16

CV H 4

Heathcote

BANBURY ROAD

A429

Castle Park

I

Kipling Av

Byron Av

Newburgh Middle School

Masefield Av

Foxes Way

Levfields Crs

Shelley Avenue

ROAD

River Avon

New Waters

2

Nursery Wood

Aylesford School

Lodge Crescent

Playbox Theatre

STRATFORD

Lodge Wood

3

22

ongbridge

Barford Wood

4

M40

WARWICK BY-PASS

Junction 14

M40

5

E

F

G

H

Debd... Farm

River Avon

Hareway Farm

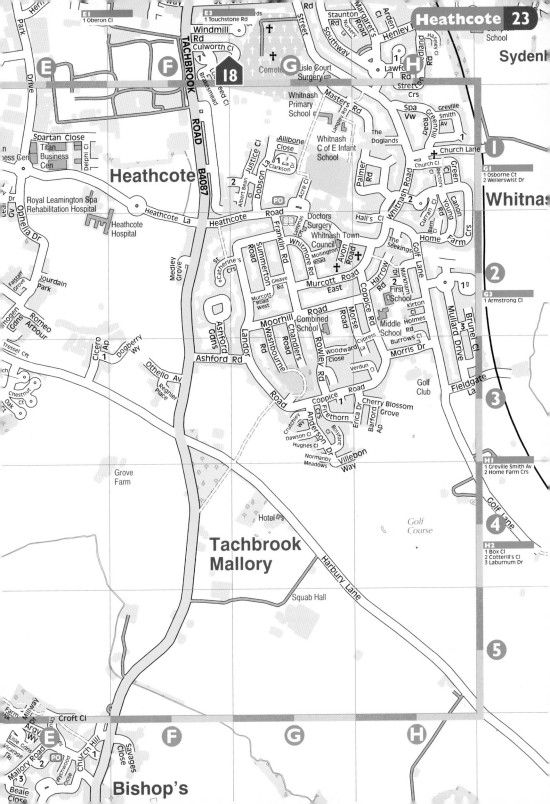

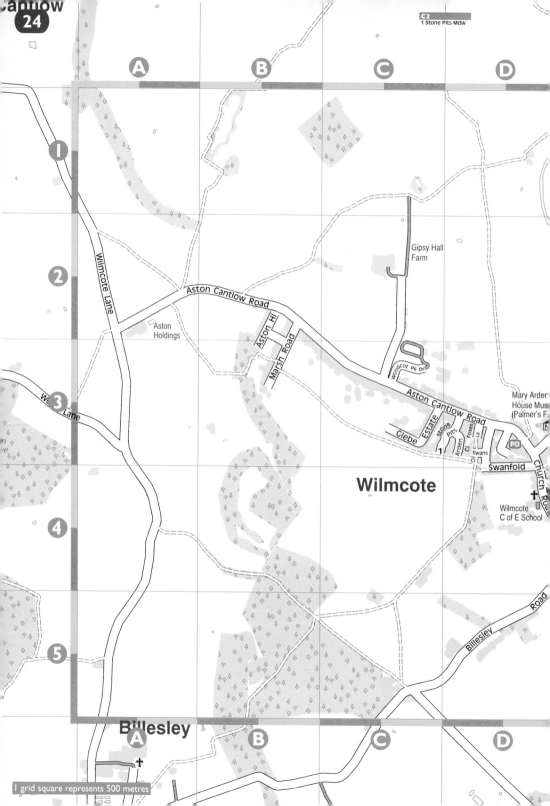

C3
1 Stone Pits Mdw

A   B   C   D

1

Wilmcote Lane

2

Gipsy Hall
Farm

Aston Cantlow Road

Aston
Holdings

Aston Hi

Marsh Road

Woodcot Pk Dr

3

We Lane

Aston Cantlow Road

Mary Arder
House Mus
(Palmer's F

Glebe

Estate

Stone

Pits

Arden
Cl

Foxes
La

Swans
Cl

PO

Swanfold

Church Road

Wilmcote

Wilmcote
C of E School

4

5

Billesley Road

A
Billesley

B

C

D

†

E   F   G   H

I

BIRMINGHAM

ROAD

Arden Hill
Farm

Pathlow

Gospel Oak Lane

Gospel
Oak

2

A3400

Featherbed   Lane

Oak
Farm

3

Rd

Wilmcote Station

BISHOPTON HILL

The
Wharf

Bishopton
Hill

4

or Dr

Wilmcote
Manor

BIRMINGHAM ROAD A3400

Churchill
Cottage

5

Manor
Farm

E   F   **26**   G   Burton
Farm   H

Stratford-upon-Avon C

Lane

26

A B **25** C D

D3
1 Curlew Cl
2 Partridge Rd
3 Pheasant Cl

D2
1 Crane Cl

Manor
Farm

Burton
Farm

I

Stratford-upon-Avon Canal

D4
1 Glebe Rd
2 Mount Pleasant
3 Sidelands Rd

Copham's Hill
Farm

2

The Ridgway

A46(T)

The
Wildmoor

Ma
C

Teal
Grove

Broadmeadow La

Quail

Bishopton Lane

Trevelyan
Dr

Sackville
Cl

Bishopton Junior
& Infant School

Ma
Co
Sc

3 ALCESTER ROAD

Shelbourne
Road

Ludford Cl

Sevincott

Glebe Rd

Mount Crs

Hillside
Road

Bishops
Close

The Ridgway

ALCESTER ROAD

Toll Ga
Cl

Lea Cl

A422

Holbrook Rd

Blacke
Ww

Alcester Rd

Manor Drive

Drayton

4

West
Green
Dr

Hathaway Green La

East Green Dr

Redlands
Crs

South Green Dr

Drayton

Drayton Manor Drive

Cottage

Ann Hathaway's
Cottage

5

Hansell
Farm

Shottery

Sho
& Ir

A B **32** C D

1 grid square represents 500 metres

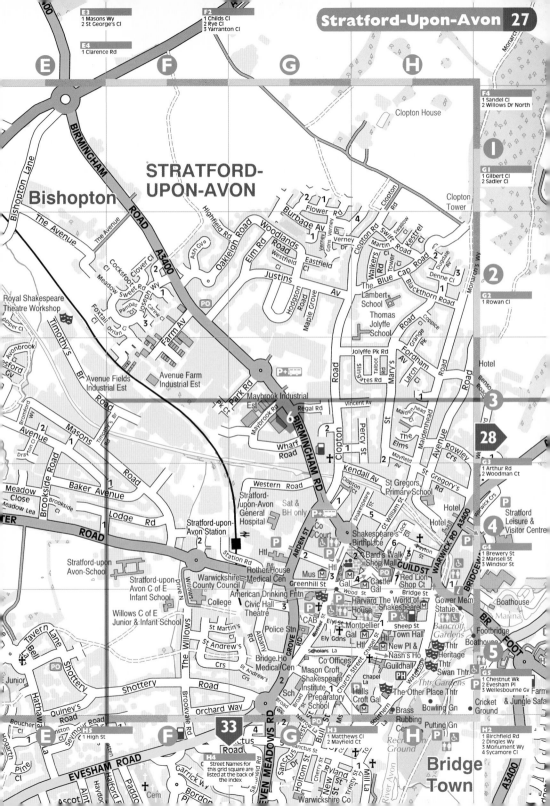

E F G H I 2 3 28 4 5 33

STRATFORD-UPON-AVON

Bishopton

Bridge Town

Clopton House

Clopton Tower

Royal Shakespeare Theatre Workshop

Avenue Fields Industrial Est

Avenue Farm Industrial Est

Maybrook Industrial Est

Stratford-upon-Avon General Hospital

Stratford-upon-Avon Station

Stratford-upon Avon-School

Warwickshire County Council

Willows C of E Junior & Infant School

Stratford-upon-Avon C of E Infant School

Rother House Medical Cen

Greenhill St

American Drinking Fntn

Civic Hall Theatre

Police Stn

Bridge Ho Medical Cen

Co Offices

Mason Croft

Shakespeare Institute

Preparatory School

Halls Croft Gal

The Other Place Thtr

Thtr Gardens

Cricket Ground

Jungle Safa

Boathouse

Marina

Footbridge

Bancroft Gardens

Gower Mem Statue

Harvard House

The World of Shakespeare

Shakespeare's Birthplace

St Gregors Primary School

Stratford Leisure & Visitor Centre

Recreation Ground

Putting Gn

Brass Rubbing Cen

Bowling Gn

EVESHAM ROAD

BIRMINGHAM ROAD A3400

River Avon

E F G H

I

von Hill
ouse

Alveston
House

Old Pasture
Farm

Ferry Lane

Avonfields
Cl

Alveston Lane

Church Lane

Alveston

River Avon

Hemingford House

WELLESBOURNE ROAD

STREET

Baraset

2

Pimlico Lane

ddington

3

30

Alveston Farm

4

Croft School

5

Pimlico Lane

Hunscote Lane

E F 35 G H

Loxley Road

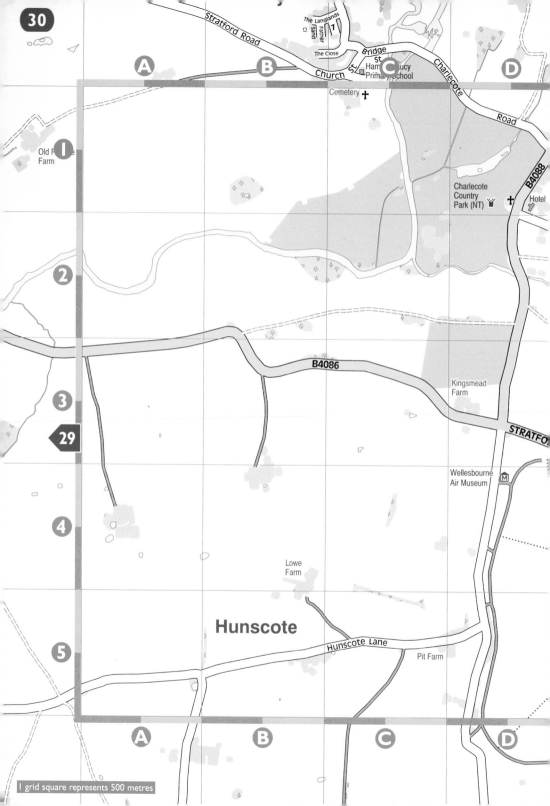

Stratford Road

The Langlands
Father's Stand
The Close
1

Bridge
St
Church St
Charlecote
Road

Hare Lucy
Primary School

A **B** **C** **D**

Cemetery †

1

Old Park Farm

B4088

Charlecote
Country
Park (NT)

Hotel
†

2

3

B4086

Kingsmead
Farm

29

STRATFO

Wellesbourne
Air Museum
M

4

Lowe
Farm

Hunscote

5

Hunscote Lane

Pit Farm

A **B** **C** **D**

32

A   **B**   **26**   **C**   **D**

Shottery

Ann Hathaway Cottage

Hansell Farm

I

Dodwell

EVESHAM ROAD B439

ROAD B439

2 Dodwell Tr Es

Luddington

stannals Cl

Avonbank Dr

3 Little Luddington Farm

Avon Valley Footpath

Monarch's Way

River Avon

Luddington

Avon Valley Footpath

Monarch's Way

4 Church Cl   Luddington Road

✝

✝

Milcote Manor Farm

5

A   **B**   **C**   **D**

Monarch's Way

Milcote Road

I grid square represents 500 metres

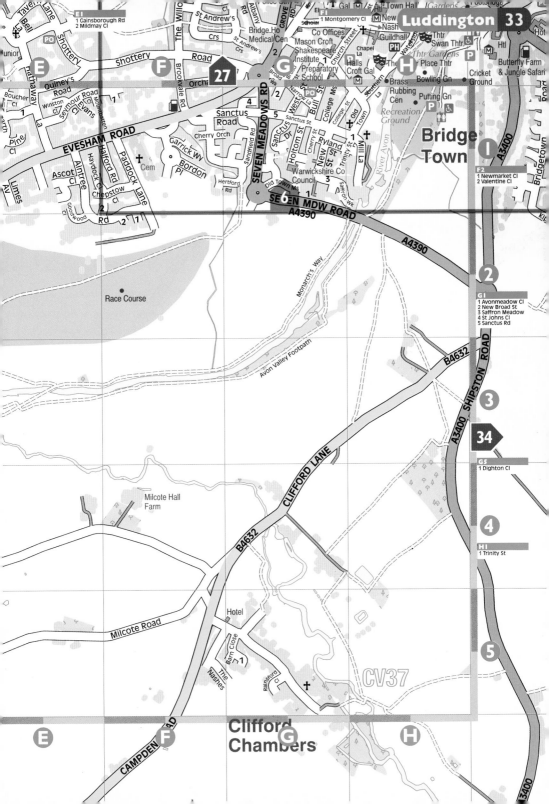

Alveston	29 F2	Drayton	26 A4	Lillington	13 F4	Shottery	26 D5
Alveston Hill	34 D1	Emscote	3 H2	Longbridge	21 E3	Stratford-upon-Avon	6 E6
Bishopton	27 E1	Guy's Cliffe	10 D5	Milverton	11 H4	Stratford-upon-Avon	27 F1
Blackdown	12 B2	Hampton Magna	15 G4	Myton	3 K6	Sydenham	19 E5
Bridge End	17 E5	Hampton on the Hill	15 E5	Old Milverton	11 E4	Tachbrook Mallory	23 F4
Bridge Town	7 G6	Haseley	8 B3	Packmores	2 A2	Tiddington	29 E3
Budbrooke	15 E3	Hatton	8 C4	Pathlow	25 G2	Warwick	2 D6
Campion Hills	19 E1	Heathcote	23 F1	Radford Semele	19 H5	Wellesbourne	31 F4
The Cape	16 B1	Hill Wootton	11 G1	Royal Leamington Spa	5 J2	Wilmcote	24 C4
Charlecote	31 E1	Hunscote	30 B5	Royal Leamington Spa	18 D1	Woodloes Park	16 B1
Cubbington	13 F1	Leek Wootton	11 E1	Sherbourne	20 B5		

USING THE STREET INDEX

Street names are listed alphabetically. Each street name is followed by its postal town or area locality, the Postcode District, the page number, and the reference to the square in which the name is found.

Example: **Abbotts St** *RLSS* CV31................5 F4 ▣

Some entries are followed by a number in a blue box. This number indicates the location of the street within the referenced grid square. The full street name is listed at the side of the map page.

GENERAL ABBREVIATIONS

ilACC	ACCESS	E	EAST	LDG	LODGE	R	RIVER
ALY	ALLEY	EMB	EMBANKMENT	LGT	LIGHT	RBT	ROUNDABOUT
AP	APPROACH	EMBY	EMBASSY	LK	LOCK	RD	ROAD
AR	ARCADE	ESP	ESPLANADE	LKS	LAKES	RDG	RIDGE
ASS	ASSOCIATION	EST	ESTATE	LNDG	LANDING	REP	REPUBLIC
AV	AVENUE	EX	EXCHANGE	LTL	LITTLE	RES	RESERVOIR
BCH	BEACH	EXPY	EXPRESSWAY	LWR	LOWER	RFC	RUGBY FOOTBALL CLUB
BLDS	BUILDINGS	EXT	EXTENSION	MAG	MAGISTRATE	RI	RISE
BND	BEND	F/O	FLYOVER	MAN	MANSIONS	RP	RAMP
BNK	BANK	FC	FOOTBALL CLUB	MD	MEAD	RW	ROW
BR	BRIDGE	FK	FORK	MDW	MEADOWS	S	SOUTH
BRK	BROOK	FLD	FIELD	MEM	MEMORIAL	SCH	SCHOOL
BTM	BOTTOM	FLDS	FIELDS	MKT	MARKET	SE	SOUTH EAST
BUS	BUSINESS	FLS	FALLS	MKTS	MARKETS	SER	SERVICE AREA
BVD	BOULEVARD	FLS	FLATS	ML	MALL	SH	SHORE
BY	BYPASS	FM	FARM	ML	MILL	SHOP	SHOPPING
CATH	CATHEDRAL	FT	FORT	MNR	MANOR	SKWY	SKYWAY
CEM	CEMETERY	FWY	FREEWAY	MS	MEWS	SMT	SUMMIT
CEN	CENTRE	FY	FERRY	MSN	MISSION	SOC	SOCIETY
CFT	CROFT	GA	GATE	MT	MOUNT	SP	SPUR
CH	CHURCH	GAL	GALLERY	MTN	MOUNTAIN	SPR	SPRING
CHA	CHASE	GDN	GARDEN	MTS	MOUNTAINS	SQ	SQUARE
CHYD	CHURCHYARD	GDNS	GARDENS	MUS	MUSEUM	ST	STREET
CIR	CIRCLE	GLD	GLADE	MWY	MOTORWAY	STN	STATION
CIRC	CIRCUS	GLN	GLEN	N	NORTH	STR	STREAM
CL	CLOSE	GN	GREEN	NE	NORTH EAST	STRD	STRAND
CLFS	CLIFFS	GND	GROUND	NW	NORTH WEST	SW	SOUTH WEST
CMP	CAMP	GRA	GRANGE	O/P	OVERPASS	TDG	TRADING
CNR	CORNER	GRG	GARAGE	OFF	OFFICE	TER	TERRACE
CO	COUNTY	GT	GREAT	ORCH	ORCHARD	THWY	THROUGHWAY
COLL	COLLEGE	GTWY	GATEWAY	OV	OVAL	TNL	TUNNEL
COM	COMMON	GV	GROVE	PAL	PALACE	TOLL	TOLLWAY
COMM	COMMISSION	HGR	HIGHER	PAS	PASSAGE	TPK	TURNPIKE
CON	CONVENT	HL	HILL	PAV	PAVILION	TR	TRACK
COT	COTTAGE	HLS	HILLS	PDE	PARADE	TRL	TRAIL
COTS	COTTAGES	HO	HOUSE	PH	PUBLIC HOUSE	TWR	TOWER
CP	CAPE	HOL	HOLLOW	PK	PARK	U/P	UNDERPASS
CPS	COPSE	HOSP	HOSPITAL	PKWY	PARKWAY	UNI	UNIVERSITY
CR	CREEK	HRB	HARBOUR	PL	PLACE	UPR	UPPER
CREM	CREMATORIUM	HTH	HEATH	PLN	PLAIN	V	VALE
CRS	CRESCENT	HTS	HEIGHTS	PLNS	PLAINS	VA	VALLEY
CSWY	CAUSEWAY	HVN	HAVEN	PLZ	PLAZA	VIAD	VIADUCT
CT	COURT	HWY	HIGHWAY	POL	POLICE STATION	VIL	VILLA
CTRL	CENTRAL	IMP	IMPERIAL	PR	PRINCE	VIS	VISTA
CTS	COURTS	IN	INLET	PREC	PRECINCT	VLG	VILLAGE
CTYD	COURTYARD	IND EST	INDUSTRIAL ESTATE	PREP	PREPARATORY	VLS	VILLAS
CUTT	CUTTINGS	INF	INFIRMARY	PRIM	PRIMARY	VW	VIEW
CV	COVE	INFO	INFORMATION	PROM	PROMENADE	W	WEST
CYN	CANYON	INT	INTERCHANGE	PRS	PRINCESS	WD	WOOD
DEPT	DEPARTMENT	IS	ISLAND	PRT	PORT	WHF	WHARF
DL	DALE	JCT	JUNCTION	PT	POINT	WK	WALK
DM	DAM	JTY	JETTY	PTH	PATH	WKS	WALKS
DR	DRIVE	KG	KING	PZ	PIAZZA	WLS	WELLS
DRO	DROVE	KNL	KNOLL	QD	QUADRANT	WY	WAY
DRY	DRIVEWAY	L	LAKE	QU	QUEEN	YD	YARD
DWGS	DWELLINGS	LA	LANE	QY	QUAY	YHA	YOUTH HOSTEL

POSTCODE TOWNS AND AREA ABBREVIATIONS

RLSS	Royal Leamington Spa south	BTACH/HAR	Bishop's Tachbrook/	WWCK	Warwick	STRAT	Stratford-upon-Avon
RLSN	Royal Leamington Spa north		Harbury	RWWCK/WEL	Rural Warwick/		
					Wellesbourne		

A

botts St RLSS CV31 5 F4 1
acia Rd RLSN CV32 4 A1
re Cl RLSS CV31 23 G1
ldingham Cl WWCK CV34 2 B1
lelaide Rd RLSN CV32 4 D3
ntree Dr RLSN CV32 13 E4
ntree Rd STRAT CV37 33 E1
bany Rd STRAT CV37 6 C4
bany Ter RLSN CV32 4 C1
bert Bean Cl RLSS CV31 23 G1
bert St RLSN CV32 3 K1
WWCK CV34 16 B3
cester Rd STRAT CV37 6 C3
STRAT CV37 26 D4
derminster Gv
RWWCK/WEL CV35 9 E5 1
ders Gv WWCK CV34 21 F1 1
derton Ms RLSS CV31 19 E4
dwick Cl RLSN CV32 12 C3
exandra Rd RLSS CV31 5 H7
libone Cl RLSS CV31 23 G1
l Saints Rd WWCK CV34 3 F1
mond Av RLSN CV32 12 B4
mond Gv WWCK CV34 17 E1 1
thorpe St RLSS CV31 5 G5
veston La STRAT CV37 29 E2
nderson Dr RLSS CV31 23 G3
nsell Rd WWCK CV34 16 B3
ntelope Gdns WWCK CV34 16 A2 1
pollo Wy WWCK CV34 17 H5
he Approach RLSS CV31 4 E6
ragon Dr RLSS CV31 4 A6
bury Cl RLSN CV32 12 C4
chery Flds WWCK CV34 16 D5 1
chery Rd RLSS CV31 4 D3
rden Cl RLSS CV31 18 D5
STRAT CV37 24 D3
WWCK CV34 3 F1
rden St STRAT CV37 6 D3
rley Ms RLSN CV32 4 B1
rlington Av RLSN CV32 12 B5
rlington Ms RLSN CV32 12 B5
rmscote Gv RWWCK/WEL CV35 8 D4
rmstrong Cl RLSS CV31 23 G3 1
rras Bvd RWWCK/WEL CV35 15 G4
rthur Rd STRAT CV37 6 D1
rundel Cl WWCK CV34 2 C2
scot Cl STRAT CV37 33 E1
scot Ride RLSN CV32 13 E4
shford Gdns RLSS CV31 23 F2
shford Rd RLSS CV31 23 F3
sh Gv STRAT CV37 27 F2
shley Crs WWCK CV34 3 H6
sh Tree Cl RWWCK/WEL CV35 31 H4
stley Cl RLSN CV32 11 H5
ston Cantlow Rd HENAR B95 24 A2
ston Hl STRAT CV37 24 B3
thena Dr RLSS CV31 17 H5
ugusta Pl RLSN CV32 4 E2
ustin Edwards Dr WWCK CV34 3 G3
ustwick Cl WWCK CV34 16 C1
venue Rd RLSS CV31 4 E4
STRAT CV37 7 F1
he Avenue STRAT CV37 27 E2
vonbank Dr STRAT CV37 32 D3
vonbrook Cl STRAT CV37 27 E3
von Crs STRAT CV37 34 C1
vondale Rd RLSN CV32 12 D3
vonfields Cl STRAT CV37 29 G2
vonlea Ri RLSN CV32 11 G5
vonmeadow Cl STRAT CV37 6 D7 1
von Rd RLSS CV31 23 G2
von St WWCK CV34 3 F4
von Valley Footpath
STRAT CV37 32 C4
ylesford St RLSS CV31 5 G7

B

ack La WWCK CV34 2 A6
addesley Cl RLSS CV31 19 F5 1
aker Av RLSS CV31 4 E7
STRAT CV37 27 E4
almoral Wy RLSN CV32 13 E1
amburgh Gv RLSN CV32 12 A4
anbury Rd BTACH/HAR CV33 22 C5
STRAT CV37 7 J6
WWCK CV34 2 C6
WWCK CV34 17 E5
ancroft Pl STRAT CV37 7 F4
ank Cft RLSS CV31 19 E5
ankfield Dr RLSN CV32 3 K1
Barcheston Dr RWWCK/WEL CV35 8 D4
Barford Ap RLSS CV31 23 H3
Barnack Dr WWCK CV34 16 C1 2
Barnard Cl RLSN CV32 13 E4 1
Barn Cl RLSS CV31 23 H2
STRAT CV37 33 G5
Barrack St WWCK CV34 2 A5
Bartlett Cl WWCK CV34 2 D5
Barton Crs RLSS CV31 19 E4 1
Barwell Cl RLSN CV32 12 B4
Basant Cl WWCK CV34 2 E4
Bath Pl RLSS CV31 5 F4
Bath St RLSS CV31 5 F4
Baxter Ct RLSS CV31 5 H5
Beaconsfield St RLSS CV31 5 J4
Beaconsfield St West
RLSS CV31 5 J3 1
Beauchamp Av RLSN CV32 18 B1
Beauchamp Gdns WWCK CV34 3 H6
Beauchamp Hl RLSN CV32 4 C1
Beauchamp Rd RLSN CV32 18 B1 1
WWCK CV34 3 G2
Beaufell Cl WWCK CV34 16 C1 3
Beaufort Av RLSN CV32 13 E2
Beaufort Cl RWWCK/WEL CV35 31 F5 1
Beaulieu Pk RLSS CV31 19 F4
Bedford Pl RLSN CV32 4 E3
Bedford St RLSN CV32 4 E1
Beech Cliffe WWCK CV34 2 D3
Beech Cl STRAT CV37 7 J5
Beech Ct STRAT CV37 7 H5
WWCK CV34 23 E3
Beeches Wk STRAT CV37 28 D3
Beech Gv WWCK CV34 3 G1
Bellam Rd RWWCK/WEL CV35 15 F3 1
Bell La STRAT CV37 27 E5
Bell Tower Ms RLSN CV32 12 B4
Belmont Dr RLSN CV32 12 C3
Bennett Dr WWCK CV34 3 H5
Benson Rd STRAT CV37 28 A3
Bentley Cl RLSN CV32 12 D4
Berenska Dr RLSN CV32 12 C5
Berrington Rd RLSS CV31 5 H6
Berwick Cl WWCK CV34 10 C5 1
Bettridge Pl
RWWCK/WEL CV35 31 G3 1
Beverley Rd RLSN CV32 17 H1
Billesley Rd STRAT CV37 24 D5
Binswood Av RLSN CV32 12 B5
Binswood St RLSN CV32 12 A5
Birch Ct WWCK CV34 22 D3
Birchfield Rd STRAT CV37 27 H2 1
Birch Gv RWWCK/WEL CV35 31 G4
Birchway Cl RLSN CV32 17 G1 1
Bird Rd WWCK CV34 22 C1
Birmingham Rd
RWWCK/WEL CV35 15 F1
STRAT CV37 6 C1
STRAT CV37 27 E1
WWCK CV34 15 H2
Bishops Cl STRAT CV37 26 D3
Bishopton Hill Birmingham Rd
STRAT CV37 25 H3
Bishopton La STRAT CV37 26 C3
Bisset Crs RLSS CV31 5 K7
Black La RLSN CV32 12 D5
Blacklow Rd WWCK CV34 17 E1
Blackthorn Rd STRAT CV37 27 H2
Blacon Wy STRAT CV37 26 D4
Blakelands Av RLSS CV31 5 K7
Blandford Rd RLSN CV32 17 G1 2
Blandford Wy
RWWCK/WEL CV35 15 G3 1
Blenheim Crs RLSS CV31 19 E5 1
Blick Rd WWCK CV34 22 C1
Blue Cap Rd STRAT CV37 27 H2
Boddington Cl RLSN CV32 13 G2
Boleyn Cl WWCK CV34 3 K6
Bolyfant Cl RLSS CV31 23 G3
Bonniksen Cl RLSS CV31 18 B5 1
Bordesley Ct RLSN CV32 12 C4
Bordon Pl STRAT CV37 6 B7
Borrowdale Dr RLSN CV32 11 G5
Boucher Cl STRAT CV37 33 E1
Bourton Dr RLSS CV31 18 D5 1
Bowers Cft RLSN CV32 12 C2
Bowling Green St WWCK CV34 16 B4 1
Box Cl RLSS CV31 23 H2 1
Braemar Rd RLSN CV32 12 D3
Brakesmead RLSS CV31 18 B5
Brandon Pde RLSN CV32 5 G2 1
Brese Av WWCK CV34 2 D1
Brewery St STRAT CV37 6 D2
Briar Cl RLSN CV32 12 D5
Bridge End WWCK CV34 2 C7
WWCK CV34 16 D5
Bridge Foot STRAT CV37 7 F3
Bridge St RWWCK/WEL CV35 31 G4
STRAT CV37 6 E4
WWCK CV34 3 J3
Bridgetown Rd STRAT CV37 7 H7
Bridgeway STRAT CV37 7 F4
Broadmeadow La STRAT CV37 26 D3
Broad St STRAT CV37 6 D5
WWCK CV34 2 D4
Broad Wk STRAT CV37 6 C5
Broadway RLSN CV32 13 G1
Bromford Wy STRAT CV37 27 E3
Brooke Cl WWCK CV34 16 D5
Brookfield Rd RLSN CV32 13 G2
Brookside Av RWWCK/WEL CV35 31 H4
Brookside Cl STRAT CV37 27 E4
Brookside Rd STRAT CV37 27 E4
Brook St WWCK CV34 2 A6
Brookvale Rd STRAT CV37 6 B5
Browning Av WWCK CV34 16 A5
Brownlow St RLSN CV32 12 C5
Broxell Cl WWCK CV34 16 A1
Brunel Cl RLSS CV31 23 H2
Brunswick St RLSS CV31 5 G6
Buckley Rd RLSN CV32 12 D5
Budbrooke Rd WWCK CV34 15 H3
Bull St STRAT CV37 6 D6
Burbage Av STRAT CV37 27 G1
Burbury Cl RLSN CV32 13 E5
Burbury Ct WWCK CV34 3 H3 1
Burford Ms RLSS CV31 19 E4 2
Burford Rd STRAT CV37 28 C5
Burges Gv WWCK CV34 2 D1
WWCK CV34 16 D1 2
Burns Av WWCK CV34 16 A5
Burns Rd RLSN CV32 12 D3
Burrows Cl RLSS CV31 23 H3
Bury Rd RLSS CV31 4 D5
The Butts WWCK CV34 2 A5
Byron Av WWCK CV34 21 E1
Byron Rd STRAT CV37 7 H7

C

Caen Cl RWWCK/WEL CV35 15 G3
Calder Wk RLSS CV31 19 E5
Camberwell Ter RLSS CV31 5 H5
Cameron Cl RLSN CV32 12 C3
Campion Gn RLSN CV32 12 C5 1
Campion Rd RLSN CV32 12 C5
Campion Ter RLSN CV32 5 H1
Canal Rd RWWCK/WEL CV35 8 C5
Canon Young Rd RLSS CV31 23 H1
Cape Rd WWCK CV34 16 B2
Capulet Dr WWCK CV34 23 E2
Carew Cl STRAT CV37 27 F2
Carters La STRAT CV37 28 D3
Cashmore Av RLSS CV31 18 B5
Cassandra Gdns WWCK CV34 22 D1 1
Castle Cl WWCK CV34 2 A7
Castle Hl WWCK CV34 2 B6
Castle La WWCK CV34 2 B6
Castle St WWCK CV34 2 A6
Caswell Rd RLSS CV31 5 K6
Cattell Rd WWCK CV34 2 A4
Cedar Cl RLSN CV32 12 C3
STRAT CV37 7 G1
Cedar Gv WWCK CV34 2 E1
Centenary Wy RLSS CV31 3 K4
Central Av RLSS CV31 5 F7
Chamberlain Cl RLSN CV32 13 G2 1
Chance Flds RLSS CV31 19 H4
Chanders Rd WWCK CV34 16 B1
Chandlers Rd RLSS CV31 23 G2
Chandos St RLSN CV32 18 B1
The Chantry WWCK CV34 3 F1
Chapel La STRAT CV37 6 E5
Chapel Rw WWCK CV34 2 B5
Chapel St RLSS CV31 5 G4
RWWCK/WEL CV35 31 G4
STRAT CV37 6 E4
WWCK CV34 2 B5
Chapman Cl RLSS CV31 19 G5
Charingworth Dr
RWWCK/WEL CV35 9 E5
Charlbury Ms RLSS CV31 19 E4
Charlecote Cl STRAT CV37 28 D4
Charlecote Flds
RWWCK/WEL CV35 31 G3 2
Charlecote Gdns RLSS CV31 19 F5
Charlecote Rd
RWWCK/WEL CV35 31 G3
Charles Gardner Rd RLSS CV31 5 F7
Charles St WWCK CV34 3 F2
Charlotte St RLSS CV31 5 F6
Charnwood Wy RLSN CV32 13 E4
Charter Approach
WWCK CV34 16 B4 2
WWCK CV34 16 B5 1
Chatsworth Gdns RLSS CV31 19 F4 1
Chatsworth Gv RLSS CV31 19 F4
Chepstow Cl STRAT CV37 33 E1
Cherry Blossom Gv RLSS CV31 23 H3
Cherry La RWWCK/WEL CV35 15 F4
Cherry Orch RWWCK/WEL CV35 31 G3
STRAT CV37 6 B6
Cherry St STRAT CV37 6 D7
WWCK CV34 2 D4
Chesford Crs WWCK CV34 3 G1
Chesford Gv STRAT CV37 27 E3
Chesham St RLSS CV31 5 K5
Chesterton Dr RLSS CV31 18 D5
Chestnut Ct WWCK CV34 23 E3
Chestnut Sq RWWCK/WEL CV35 31 G4
Chestnut Wk STRAT CV37 6 D5
Cheviot Ri RLSN CV32 13 E4 2
Chichester La RWWCK/WEL CV35 15 E4
Childs Cl STRAT CV37 27 F2 1
Church Cl RLSS CV31 23 H1
STRAT CV37 32 A4
Church End RLSS CV31 19 G4
Church Hl RLSN CV32 4 C2
RLSN CV32 13 G2
Church La RLSN CV32 12 C4
RLSN CV32 13 G1
RLSS CV31 23 H1
STRAT CV37 26 D4
STRAT CV37 29 F2
Church Lees BTACH/HAR CV33 23 E5
Church Pth RWWCK/WEL CV35 15 F4 1
Church Rd STRAT CV37 24 D3
Church St RLSS CV31 5 G4
RWWCK/WEL CV35 31 G4
STRAT CV37 6 D5
WWCK CV34 2 A6
Church Ter RLSS CV31 5 G4
Church Wk RLSS CV31 5 F4
RWWCK/WEL CV35 31 G4
Cicero Ap WWCK CV34 23 E3
Clapham Sq RLSS CV31 5 J5
Clapham St RLSS CV31 5 J6
Clapham Ter RLSS CV31 5 J5
Clare Cl RLSN CV32 13 E5
Claremont Rd RLSS CV31 5 F7
Clarence Rd STRAT CV37 27 E4 1
Clarence St RLSS CV31 5 G6
Clarence Ter RLSN CV32 4 E1 1
Clarendon Av RLSN CV32 4 D1
RLSN CV32 18 B1
Clarendon Crs RLSN CV32 18 A1
Clarendon Pl RLSN CV32 4 D1
Clarendon Sq RLSN CV32 18 B1
Clarendon St RLSN CV32 12 C5
Clarkson Dr RLSS CV31 23 G1
Cleeves Av RLSS CV31 3 K5
Clemens St RLSS CV31 5 G5
Cliffe Rd RLSN CV32 4 B1
RLSN CV32 17 H1
Cliffe Wy WWCK CV34 2 D2
Clifford La STRAT CV37 33 H3
Clinton Av RWWCK/WEL CV35 15 G3 2
Clinton St RLSS CV31 5 G4
Cloister Crofts RLSN CV32 12 B4
Cloister Wy RLSN CV32 12 B4
Clopton Ct STRAT CV37 6 D2
Clopton Rd STRAT CV37 6 D2
STRAT CV37 27 H1
The Close RLSS CV31 5 H7
Clover Cl STRAT CV37 27 F2
Cobden Av RLSS CV31 19 E5
Cockermouth Cl RLSN CV32 11 H5
Cocksfoot Cl STRAT CV37 27 F2
Cocksparrow St WWCK CV34 16 B4 3
Colbourne Grove Dr
RLSN CV32 11 H5 1
College Dr RLSN CV32 12 B5
College La STRAT CV37 6 D6
College Ms STRAT CV37 6 D6
College St STRAT CV37 6 D6
Collins Rd WWCK CV34 17 H5
Combroke Gv RWWCK/WEL CV35 9 E5
Commainge Cl WWCK CV34 16 B3
Compton Cl RLSN CV32 13 E5
Comyn St RLSN CV32 18 D1 1
Congreve Cl WWCK CV34 10 D5 1
Conifer Gv RLSS CV31 18 C5
Coningsby Cl RLSS CV31 19 E4 3
Conway Rd RLSN CV32 4 A2
Cooke Cl WWCK CV34 10 D5 2
Coppice Cl STRAT CV37 27 H2
Coppice Rd RLSS CV31 23 H2
Copps Rd RLSN CV32 4 B2
Corbison Cl WWCK CV34 16 B1
Cordelia Gn WWCK CV34 22 D2
Cornwall Cl WWCK CV34 2 C2
Cornwall Pl RLSN CV32 4 B1

Corston Ms *RLSS* CV31 .... 19 E4
Cosford Cl *RLSN* CV32 .... 12 D4
Coten End *WWCK* CV34 .... 2 D5
Cottage Cl *RLSS* CV31 .... 19 E4
Cottage La *STRAT* CV37 .... 26 D5
Cotterill's Cl *STRAT* CV31 .... 23 H2 ⬛
Cotton Mill Spinney *RLSN* CV32 ...... 13 G3
Coughton Dr *RLSS* CV31 .... 19 F5
Court St *RLSS* CV31 .... 5 G5
Coventry Rd *WWCK* CV34 .... 2 D3
    WWCK CV34 .... 11 E5
Cowdray Cl *RLSS* CV31 .... 19 E3
Cowper Cl *WWCK* CV34 .... 10 C5
    WWCK CV34 .... 16 D1 ⬛
Craig Cl *RLSS* CV31 .... 18 D5 ⬛
Crane Cl *STRAT* CV37 .... 26 D2 ⬛
    WWCK CV34 .... 16 B1
Cranmer Gv *WWCK* CV34 .... 22 D2
Crawford Cl *RLSN* CV32 .... 12 D3
The Crest *RLSN* CV32 .... 13 E4
Croft Cl *WWCK* CV34 .... 3 J5
Cromer Rd *RLSN* CV32 .... 12 D5
Crompton St *WWCK* CV34 .... 16 B4
Cross Fields Rd *WWCK* CV34 .... 2 C2
Cross La *RLSN* CV32 .... 13 G3
Cross Rd *RLSN* CV32 .... 4 B1
Cross St *RLSN* CV32 .... 5 F4
    WWCK CV34 .... 2 C5 ⬛
Crown Ter *RLSS* CV31 .... 5 F5
Crown Wy *RLSN* CV32 .... 12 D4
Crutchley Wy *RLSS* CV31 .... 23 G3
Cubbington Rd *RLSN* CV32 .... 12 C4
    RLSN CV32 .... 13 E3
Culworth Cl *RLSS* CV31 .... 18 B5 ⬛
Cumberland Crs *RLSN* CV32 .... 13 E4 ⬛
Cumming St *RLSS* CV31 .... 5 G5 ⬛
Cundall Cl *RLSS* CV31 .... 5 K7
Curlew Cl *STRAT* CV37 .... 26 D3 ⬛
Curlieu Cl *RWWCK/WEL* CV35 .. 15 G4 ⬛
Curran Cl *RLSS* CV31 .... 23 H2
Cypress La *RLSS* CV31 .... 23 H3

D

Dale Av *STRAT* CV37 .... 7 K6
Dale Cl *WWCK* CV34 .... 3 F2
Dale St *RLSN* CV32 .... 4 D2
Daly Av *RWWCK/WEL* CV35 .... 15 F4
Damson Rd *RWWCK/WEL* CV35 .. 15 F4 ⬛
Danesbury Crs *RLSS* CV31 .... 19 F4
Daniell Rd *RWWCK/WEL* CV35 .... 31 G3
Dark La *STRAT* CV37 .... 28 D3
Davidson Av *RLSS* CV31 .... 5 H5
Davis Cl *RLSN* CV32 .... 11 H5
Dawson Cl *RLSN* CV32 .... 23 G3
Deansway *WWCK* CV34 .... 16 B1
Deerpark Dr *WWCK* CV34 .... 16 B2
Delamere Wy *RLSN* CV32 .... 13 E3
Delphi Cl *RLSS* CV31 .... 23 E1
Denby Cl *RLSN* CV32 .... 13 E5
Denne Cl *STRAT* CV37 .... 27 H2
Dennett Cl *WWCK* CV34 .... 10 D5 ⬛
Denville Rd *RLSN* CV32 .... 12 C4
Dereham Ct *RLSN* CV32 .... 12 C4
Derwent Cl *RLSN* CV32 .... 17 H1 ⬛
Dickens Rd *WWCK* CV34 .... 3 G2
Dighton St *STRAT* CV37 .... 33 G5 ⬛
Dingles Wy *STRAT* CV37 .... 27 H2 ⬛
Dobson La *RLSS* CV31 .... 23 G1
Dodd Av *WWCK* CV34 .... 3 J5
Dogberry Wy *WWCK* CV34 .... 23 F3
The Doglands *RLSS* CV31 .... 23 H1
Dongan Rd *WWCK* CV34 .... 2 A4
Dorchester Av
    CV35 .... 15 F4
Dormer Pl *RLSN* CV32 .... 4 E3
Dorsington Cl *RWWCK/WEL* CV35 ...... 9 F4
Drayton Av *STRAT* CV37 .... 26 D3
Drayton Cl *STRAT* CV37 .... 27 E3
Drayton Ct *WWCK* CV34 .... 10 C5 ⬛
Drayton Manor Dr *STRAT* CV37 ...... 26 A4
Dudley Gn *RLSS* CV31 .... 12 D5
Dugdale Av *STRAT* CV37 .... 27 H2
Duke St *RLSN* CV32 .... 5 H1
Dunblane Dr *RLSN* CV32 .... 13 E2
Duxford Cl *RWWCK/WEL* CV35 .. 31 F5 ⬛

E

Eagle St *RLSS* CV31 .... 5 H6
Earl Rivers Av *WWCK* CV34 .... 22 D2
Earl St *RLSN* CV32 .... 18 C1
East Dene *RLSN* CV32 .... 12 D5
Eastfield Cl *STRAT* CV37 .... 27 G2

Eastfield Rd *RLSN* CV32 .... 5 H2
East Green Dr *STRAT* CV37 .... 26 D4
East Gv *RLSS* CV31 .... 5 G6
Eastley Crs *WWCK* CV34 .... 15 H2
Eastnor Gv *RLSS* CV31 .... 5 K5
Eaton Cl *RLSN* CV32 .... 11 H5
Eborall Cl *WWCK* CV34 .... 10 C5
Ebrington Dr *RWWCK/WEL* CV35 ...... 9 F5
Edinburgh Crs *RLSS* CV31 .... 4 E6
Edmondes Cl *WWCK* CV34 .... 2 C1
Edmondscote Rd *RLSN* CV32 .... 4 A3
Edward St *RLSN* CV32 .... 3 K1
    WWCK CV34 .... 16 B3 ⬛
Elan Cl *RLSN* CV32 .... 13 E4
Eliot Cl *WWCK* CV34 .... 10 C5
Elizabeth Ct *WWCK* CV34 .... 3 H7
Elizabeth Rd *RLSS* CV31 .... 4 D7
Elliot Dr *RWWCK/WEL* CV35 .... 31 F4
Elliston Gv *RLSS* CV31 .... 19 E4
Elm Bank Cl *RLSN* CV32 .... 12 C3
Elm Rd *RLSN* CV32 .... 12 D4
    STRAT CV37 .... 27 G2
The Elms *RWWCK/WEL* CV35 .... 11 E1
    STRAT CV37 .... 6 E1
Elton Cl *RLSN* CV32 .... 13 E5
Ely Gdns *STRAT* CV37 .... 6 D4
Ely St *STRAT* CV37 .... 6 D4
Emerald Wy *RLSS* CV31 .... 18 B5 ⬛
Emmott Dr *RLSN* CV31 .... 18 D5
Emscote Rd *WWCK* CV34 .... 3 F4
Endsleigh Gdns *RLSS* CV31 .... 5 K7
England Crs *RLSS* CV31 .... 4 D5
Ennerdale Cl *RLSN* CV32 .... 11 H5
Enright Cl *RLSN* CV32 .... 12 A5
Epping Wy *RLSN* CV32 .... 13 E3
Epsom Rd *RLSN* CV32 .... 13 E3
Erica Dr *RLSS* CV31 .... 23 H3
Eton Rd *STRAT* CV37 .... 7 K6
Ettington Cl *RWWCK/WEL* CV35 .. 31 G5
Ettington Rd *RWWCK/WEL* CV35 .. 31 G5
Europa Wy *RLSS* CV31 .... 4 B6
    WWCK CV34 .... 22 C1
Euston Pl *RLSN* CV32 .... 5 F3
Evans Cl *STRAT* CV37 .... 33 E1
Evenlode Cl *STRAT* CV37 .... 7 K6
Evesham Pl *STRAT* CV37 .... 6 C5
Exhall Cl *STRAT* CV37 .... 34 C1 ⬛
Exham Cl *WWCK* CV34 .... 16 C1 ⬛
Exmoor Dr *RLSN* CV32 .... 13 E3 ⬛
Eyffler Cl *WWCK* CV34 .... 16 B3 ⬛

F

Fairhurst Dr *RLSN* CV32 .... 12 A4
Fairlawn Cl *RLSN* CV32 .... 4 A1
The Fairways *RLSS* CV32 .... 11 H5
Falstaff Gv *WWCK* CV34 .... 23 E2
Farley St *RLSS* CV31 .... 5 J4
Farm Av *STRAT* CV37 .... 27 F3
Farm Rd *RLSN* CV32 .... 12 D4
Farm Wk *BTACH/HAR* CV33 .... 23 E5
Farrington Cl *RWWCK/WEL* CV35 .. 31 F5
Featherbed La *STRAT* CV37 .... 6 D3
Fell Gv *RLSN* CV32 .... 12 C3
Fellmore Gv *RLSS* CV31 .... 19 E3 ⬛
Fernhill Dr *RLSN* CV32 .... 5 J1
Ferry La *STRAT* CV37 .... 29 G1
Field Barn Rd *RWWCK/WEL* CV35 .. 15 F3
Field Cl *WWCK* CV34 .... 3 G4
Fieldgate La *RLSS* CV31 .... 23 H3
Field Head La *WWCK* CV34 .... 3 H6
Firethorn Crs *RLSS* CV31 .... 23 G3
Fisher's Ct *WWCK* CV34 .... 21 F1 ⬛
Flavel Crs *RLSS* CV31 .... 4 E5
Fletchers Wy *RWWCK/WEL* CV35 .. 31 F4
Flower Rd *STRAT* CV37 .... 27 G1
Fordham Av *STRAT* CV37 .... 27 H5
Forfield Pl *RLSS* CV31 .... 5 G4
Fosberry Cl *WWCK* CV34 .... 3 G3
Fountain Gdns
    RWWCK/WEL CV35 .... 31 G3 ⬛
Foxes La *STRAT* CV37 .... 24 D3
Foxes Wy *WWCK* CV34 .... 21 F1
Foxtail Cl *STRAT* CV37 .... 27 E2
Frances Av *WWCK* CV34 .... 3 F4
Frances Havergal Cl *RLSS* CV31 ...... 5 F6
Franklin Rd *RLSS* CV31 .... 23 G2
Freemans Cl *RLSN* CV32 .... 18 A1
Friars St *WWCK* CV34 .... 16 B4
Friary Cl *RWWCK/WEL* CV35 .. 15 F4 ⬛
Frost Rd *RWWCK/WEL* CV35 .. 31 G3
Fryer Av *RLSN* CV32 .... 12 A5

G

Gainsborough Dr *RLSS* CV31 .... 19 E3
Gainsborough Rd *STRAT* CV37 .. 33 E1 ⬛
Gallows Hl *WWCK* CV34 .... 17 F5
Garden Ct *WWCK* CV34 .... 2 B5
The Gardens *RLSS* CV31 .... 19 G5
Garrick Wy *STRAT* CV37 .... 6 B6
Garway Cl *RLSN* CV32 .... 12 B3
Gas St *RLSS* CV31 .... 5 F5
Gaveston Cl *WWCK* CV34 .... 2 D2
Gaveston Rd *RLSN* CV32 .... 18 A1
George Rd *WWCK* CV34 .... 3 F2
George St *RLSS* CV31 .... 5 G4
Gerrard St *WWCK* CV34 .... 2 B6
Giffard Wy *WWCK* CV34 .... 16 C1 ⬛
Gilbert Cl *STRAT* CV37 .... 27 G1 ⬛
Girvan Gv *RLSN* CV32 .... 13 E2
Gisburn Cl *WWCK* CV34 .... 2 C1
    WWCK CV34 .... 16 D1
Gleave Rd *RLSS* CV31 .... 23 G2
Glebe Est *STRAT* CV37 .... 24 C3
Glebe Pl *RLSS* CV31 .... 5 K4
Glebe Rd *STRAT* CV37 .... 26 D4 ⬛
Gleeson Dr *WWCK* CV34 .... 16 C1 ⬛
Gloucester St *RLSS* CV31 .... 5 F4
Glover Cl *WWCK* CV34 .... 20 D1 ⬛
Godfrey Cl *RLSN* CV32 .... 19 G5
Goldsmith Av *WWCK* CV34 .... 16 A5
Golf La *RLSS* CV31 .... 23 H2
Goodfellow St *RLSN* CV32 .... 3 K1
Goodwood Cl *STRAT* CV37 .... 33 E1
Gordon St *RLSS* CV31 .... 5 H4
Gospel Oak La *STRAT* CV37 .... 25 H2
Gould Rd *RWWCK/WEL* CV35 .. 15 G3
Grand Union Canal Wk *RLSS* CV31 .. 3 K5
    RLSS CV31 .... 19 G4
    RWWCK/WEL CV35 .... 8 A5
    RWWCK/WEL CV35 .... 15 G2
    WWCK CV34 .... 2 A1
Grange Cl *WWCK* CV34 .... 3 J3
Grange Gdns *RWWCK/WEL* CV35 .. 31 G4
Grange Pk *STRAT* CV37 .... 27 H5
Grange Rd *RLSN* CV32 .... 12 C4
The Grange *RLSS* CV31 .... 3 J5
Granville Rd *RWWCK/WEL* CV35 .. 31 F4
Granville St *RLSN* CV32 .... 12 C5
Grassington Av *WWCK* CV34 .... 16 D1
Greatheed Rd *RLSN* CV32 .... 18 A1
Great William St *STRAT* CV37 .... 6 E3
Greaves Cl *WWCK* CV34 .... 3 K5
Green Cl *RLSS* CV31 .... 23 H1
Greenhill Rd *RLSS* CV31 .... 23 H1
Greenhill St *STRAT* CV37 .... 6 D3
Green La *WWCK* CV34 .... 2 B3
The Green *RWWCK/WEL* CV35 .. 8 A3 ⬛
Greenway *WWCK* CV34 .... 2 B1
The Greenways *RLSN* CV32 .. 12 D4 ⬛
Grenfell Cl *RLSS* CV31 .... 19 F4 ⬛
Gresham Av *RLSS* CV31 .... 12 D5
Gresham Pl *RLSN* CV32 .... 12 D5
The Greswoldes *RLSS* CV31 .... 19 H4
Greville Rd *WWCK* CV34 .... 3 G1
Greville Smith Av *RLSS* CV31 .. 23 H1 ⬛
Griffin Rd *RLSS* CV31 .... 3 K5
Grosvenor Rd *RLSN* CV32 .... 18 C5
Grouse Cl *STRAT* CV37 .... 26 D2
Grove Cft *RWWCK/WEL* CV35 .. 15 E5
Grove Pk *RWWCK/WEL* CV35 .. 14 D4
Grove Pl *RLSS* CV31 .... 5 G6
Grove Rd *RLSN* CV32 .... 6 D4
Grove St *RLSN* CV32 .... 4 D1
Guild St *STRAT* CV37 .... 6 E3
Gulistan Rd *RLSN* CV32 .... 4 C1
Gulliman's Wy *RLSS* CV31 .... 19 F4
Gundry Cl *RLSS* CV31 .... 5 H5
Gunnery Ter *RLSN* CV32 .... 4 B1
Guy Pl East *RLSN* CV32 .... 5 F1
Guy Pl West *RLSN* CV32 .... 5 F1
Guy's Cliffe Av *RLSN* CV32 .... 11 G5
Guy's Cliffe Rd *RLSN* CV32 .... 4 C2
Guy's Cliffe Ter *WWCK* CV34 .... 2 D4
Guy's Cross Park Rd *WWCK* CV34 .. 2 C2
Guy St *WWCK* CV34 .... 2 D4

H

Haddon Rd *RLSN* CV32 .... 12 D5
Hadrian Cl *STRAT* CV37 .... 12 D3
Halford Rd *STRAT* CV37 .... 33 E1
Hallfields *RLSS* CV31 .... 19 G5
Hall Av *RLSN* CV32 .... 18 B1
Hall's Cl *RLSS* CV31 .... 23 H2

Hamilton Rd *RLSS* CV31 19
    STRAT CV37 28
Hamilton Ter *RLSS* CV32 5
Hammond Gn *RWWCK/WEL* CV35.. 31
Hampdon Wy *RWWCK/WEL* CV35.. 31
Hampton Cft
    RWWCK/WEL CV35 .... 20 A
Hampton Rd *RWWCK/WEL* CV35.. 15
    WWCK CV34 15
Hampton St *WWCK* CV34 16
Hanworth Cl *RLSN* CV32 12
Hanworth Rd *WWCK* CV34 16
Harbury La *BTACH/HAR* CV33 22
    WWCK CV34 22
Harmar Cl *WWCK* CV34 22
Harriott Dr *WWCK* CV34 22
Harris Cl *RWWCK/WEL* CV35 31
Harris Rd *WWCK* CV34 16
Harrow Rd *RLSS* CV31 18
Haseley Cl *RLSS* CV31 18
Hastings Rd *RWWCK/WEL* CV35 .. 31
Hathaway Dr *WWCK* CV34 10
Hathaway Green La *STRAT* CV37 .. 26
Hathaway La *STRAT* CV37 26
Hatherell Rd *RLSS* CV31 19
Hatton Cl *RWWCK/WEL* CV35.. 8
Hawkes Dr *WWCK* CV34 22
Hawthorn Rd *RLSS* CV31 4
Haydock Cl *STRAT* CV37 33
Hayle Av *WWCK* CV34 2
Hayward Cl *RWWCK/WEL* CV35 .. 15 F
Hazel Cl *RLSN* CV32 12
Heathcote La *RLSS* CV31 23
    WWCK CV34 17
    WWCK CV34 22
Heathcote Rd *RLSS* CV31 23
Heathcote Wy *WWCK* CV34 22
Heather Cl *STRAT* CV37 27
Heath Ter *RLSN* CV32 2
Hebden Av *WWCK* CV34 2
Heemstede La *RLSN* CV32 12
Hellidon Cl *RLSN* CV32 12
Helmsdale Rd *RLSN* CV32 12
Hemmings Cl *RLSS* CV31 .... 19 G5
Henley Rd *RLSS* CV31 18
Henley St *STRAT* CV37 .... 6 E
Hermes Cl *RLSS* CV31 18
Heron La *STRAT* CV37 26
Hertford Rd *STRAT* CV37 6
Hicks Cl *WWCK* CV34 .... 10 C5
Hidcote Cl *RLSS* CV31 .... 19 E5
Highcroft Crs *RLSN* CV32 3
Highdown Rd *RLSS* CV31 5
Highfield Ter *RLSN* CV32 27
Highfield Ter *RLSN* CV32 4
Highland Rd *RLSN* CV32 12
Highlands Cl *WWCK* CV34 2
High St *RLSN* CV32 5
    RLSS CV31 5
    STRAT CV37 6
    WWCK CV34 2
High View Rd *RLSN* CV32 13
Hill Cl *RLSN* CV32 12
Hill Crest *RLSN* CV32 13
Hillside Rd *STRAT* CV37 26
Hill St *RLSN* CV32 5
    WWCK CV34 3
Hill Wootton Rd
    RWWCK/WEL CV35 11
    RWWCK/WEL CV35 11
Hind Cl *WWCK* CV34 10
Hitchman Ms *RLSS* CV31 .... 18 C5
Hitchman Rd *RLSS* CV31 18
Hockley Rd *RWWCK/WEL* CV35 .. 8
Hodgson Rd *STRAT* CV37 .... 27 C
Hogarth Rd *STRAT* CV37 33
Holbrook Rd *STRAT* CV37 26
Holioak Dr *WWCK* CV34 .... 3 C
The Holloway *WWCK* CV34 .... 16 B4
Holly Ldg *RWWCK/WEL* CV35 .. 31 G4
Holly St *RLSN* CV32 5
Holly Wk *RLSN* CV32 5
Holmes Rd *RLSS* CV31 23
The Holt *RLSN* CV32 12
Holtom St *STRAT* CV37 6
Home Farm *RWWCK/WEL* CV35 .. 11
Home Farm Crs *RLSS* CV31 .... 23 H1
Hopkins Wy *RWWCK/WEL* CV35 .. 31 C
Hopper's La
    RWWCK/WEL CV35 .... 31 G3
Hopton Crofts *RLSN* CV32 11
Hotchkiss Cl *RWWCK/WEL* CV35.. 31 F
Huddisdon Cl *WWCK* CV34 .... 2 C
Hughes Cl *RLSS* CV31 .... 23 C
    WWCK CV34 .... 10 B
Humphris St *WWCK* CV34 .... 3 C
Hunscote La *STRAT* CV37 .... 29 C
Hunt Cl *RWWCK/WEL* CV35 .. 15 F4

...unts Rd *STRAT* CV37 .... **7** H6
...urlbutt Rd *WWCK* CV34 ...... **22** C1
...urley Cl *RLSN* CV32 .... **12** C5
...yde Pl *RLSN* CV32 .... **4** C2

I

...ex Ct *WWCK* CV34 .... **2** E4
...mington Cl *RWWCK/WEL* CV35 .. **8** D5 🔲
...inogen Gdns *WWCK* CV34 ...... **23** E2
...nchford Av *WWCK* CV34 .... **10** C5
...inglewood Cl *RLSN* CV32 ...... **12** C4
...nage Cl *RLSS* CV31 .... **5** H3

J

...ckson Cl *RWWCK/WEL* CV35 ...... **15** F4
...smine Gv *RLSN* CV32 .... **12** C5
...nton Rd *RLSN* CV31 .... **5** J7
...ohn St *RLSN* CV32 .... **4** E2
...*STRAT* CV37 .... **6** E3
...olyffe Park Rd *STRAT* CV37 ...... **27** H3
...oseph Way *STRAT* CV37 .... **27** F2
...ourdain Pk *WWCK* CV34 .... **23** E2
...oyce Pool *WWCK* CV34 .... **2** A5 🔲
...iry St *WWCK* CV34 .... **2** A6
...istice Cl *RLSS* CV31 .... **23** G1
...istins Av *STRAT* CV37 .... **27** G2

K

...eats Rd *STRAT* CV37 .... **7** H7
...eir Cl *RLSN* CV32 .... **12** C5
...eith Rd *RLSN* CV32 .... **12** D3
...elvin Rd *RLSN* CV32 .... **12** D2
...emp Cl *WWCK* CV34 .... **3** F4
...empton Crs *RLSN* CV32 .... **13** E3
...endal Av *STRAT* CV37 .... **11** G5
...endall Av *STRAT* CV37 .... **6** D2
...enilworth Rd *RLSN* CV32 .... **12** B5
...*RLSN* CV32 .... **13** E1
...*RLSN* CV32 .... **18** B1
...enilworth Rd *RLSS* CV31 .... **5** F1
...ennan Av *RLSS* CV31 .... **4** E5
...estrel Cl *STRAT* CV37 .... **27** H2
...eswick Gn *RLSN* CV32 .... **17** H1
...ettlewell Cl *WWCK* CV34 .... **16** C1
...ilby Gv *RLSS* CV31 .... **19** E5 🔲
...idwick Wy *WWCK* CV34 .... **2** B1 🔲
...iln Cl *RLSN* CV32 .... **12** C5
...insey Av *WWCK* CV34 .... **2** B1
...ineton Rd *RWWCK/WEL* CV35 ...... **31** H5
...ingland Dr *STRAT* CV37 .... **17** G1
...ingshurst *RLSS* CV31 .... **19** G4
...ing St *RLSN* CV32 .... **5** G1
...ingsway *RLSS* CV31 .... **4** E6
...inross Rd *RLSN* CV32 .... **12** D3
...ipling Av *RLSS* CV31 .... **21** E1
...ipling Rd *STRAT* CV37 .... **34** A2
...irby Av *WWCK* CV34 .... **16** D1
...irton Cl *RLSS* CV31 .... **23** H2
...issing Tree La *STRAT* CV37 ...... **7** H7
...ites Cl *WWCK* CV34 .... **10** C5
...ites Nest La *RWWCK/WEL* CV35 .... **8** D2
...nightcote Dr *RLSN* CV32 .... **4** C3
...nightley Cl *RLSN* CV32 .... **13** G2
...nights La *STRAT* CV37 .... **28** D3
...noll Dr *WWCK* CV34 .... **10** C5

L

...aburnum Dr *RLSS* CV31 .... **23** H2 🔲
...aburnum Gv *WWCK* CV34 .... **17** F1
...acell Cl *WWCK* CV34 .... **16** B1
...adycroft *RLSN* CV32 .... **13** G2
...akin Cl *WWCK* CV34 .... **2** C3
...akin Rd *WWCK* CV34 .... **2** C2
...ambourn Crs *RLSS* CV31 .... **19** E4
...amintone Dr *RLSN* CV32 .... **11** G5
...ammas Cft *RLSS* CV31 .... **23** G2
...andor Rd *RLSS* CV31 .... **23** G2
...*WWCK* CV34 .... **16** B2 🔲
...angcliffe Av *WWCK* CV34 .... **17** F1
...angdale Rd *RLSN* CV32 .... **13** F4
...angley Rd *RLSS* CV31 .... **23** G1
...ansdowne Circ *RLSN* CV32 ...... **5** H1 🔲
...ansdowne Crs *RLSN* CV32 .... **5** G1
...ansdowne Rd *RLSN* CV32 .... **5** G1 🔲
...ansdowne St *RLSN* CV32 .... **5** G1

Larch Cl *STRAT* CV37 .... **27** H3
Larch Gv *WWCK* CV34 .... **17** E1 🔲
Lawford Rd *RLSS* CV31 .... **18** D5
Lawson Av *STRAT* CV37 .... **28** D3
Lay Gdns *RLSS* CV31 .... **19** G5
Lea Cl *STRAT* CV37 .... **26** C3
Leam Rd *RLSS* CV31 .... **3** K5
Leam St *RLSS* CV31 .... **5** J4
Leam Ter *RLSS* CV31 .... **5** K3
Lear Gv *WWCK* CV34 .... **23** E2
Ledbrook Rd *RLSN* CV32 .... **13** F2
Ledbury Rd *RLSS* CV31 .... **19** E4
Lee Cl *WWCK* CV34 .... **10** C5
Lee Rd *RLSS* CV31 .... **4** D5
Leicester St *RLSS* CV31 .... **18** C1
Leighton Cl *RLSN* CV32 .... **13** E3
Lewis Rd *RLSS* CV31 .... **19** G5
Leyburn Cl *WWCK* CV34 .... **2** C1 🔲
Leycester Cl *WWCK* CV34 .... **2** A7 🔲
Leyfields Crs *WWCK* CV34 .... **21** F1
Lilac Gv *WWCK* CV34 .... **17** E1
Lillington Av *RLSN* CV32 .... **12** B5
Lillington Cl *RLSN* CV32 .... **12** C5
Lillington Rd *RLSN* CV32 .... **12** C5
Lime Av *RLSN* CV32 .... **12** C3
Limes Av *STRAT* CV37 .... **27** G2
Lincoln Cl *WWCK* CV34 .... **16** C1 🔲
Linden Av *RWWCK/WEL* CV35 .... **31** H4 🔲
Linden Cl *WWCK* CV34 .... **10** C5
Linen St *WWCK* CV34 .... **16** B4
Linkway *RLSS* CV31 .... **4** C6
Livery St *RLSN* CV32 .... **5** F2
Llewellyn Rd *RLSS* CV31 .... **5** G7
Lloyd Cl *RWWCK/WEL* CV35 ...... **15** F4 🔲
Lock Cl *STRAT* CV37 .... **6** E3
Lockheed Cl *RLSS* CV31 .... **18** B5
Lock La *WWCK* CV34 .... **16** B1
Lodge Crs *WWCK* CV34 .... **21** F1
Longfellow Av *STRAT* CV37 ...... **21** E1 🔲
Longfield Rd *RLSS* CV31 .... **5** K7
Longleat Gv *RLSS* CV31 .... **19** E4
Lonsdale Rd *RLSN* CV32 .... **12** D3
Loveday Cl *STRAT* CV37 .... **12** A5
Lower Av *RLSS* CV31 .... **5** F1
Lower Cape *WWCK* CV34 .... **16** B2
Lower Leam St *RLSS* CV31 .... **5** J3
Lower Villiers St *RLSN* CV32 .... **18** C1
Lowes Av *WWCK* CV34 .... **16** C1
Lowes La *RWWCK/WEL* CV35 .... **31** G5
Loxley Cl *RWWCK/WEL* CV35 .... **31** F5
Loxley Rd *RWWCK/WEL* CV35 .... **31** F5
...*STRAT* CV37 .... **7** H4
Loxley Wy *RLSN* CV32 .... **12** C4
Luddington Rd *STRAT* CV37 ..... **32** A4
Ludford Cl *STRAT* CV37 .... **26** C3
Lysander Cl *RWWCK/WEL* CV35 .. **31** F5 🔲
Lyster Cl *WWCK* CV34 .... **15** H2 🔲
Lythall Cl *RLSS* CV31 .... **19** H5
Lyttelton Rd *WWCK* CV34 .... **2** A2

M

Macbeth Ap *WWCK* CV34 .... **22** D1
Maidenhead Cl *STRAT* CV37 ..... **6** E1
Maidenhead Rd *STRAT* CV37 .... **7** F2
Main St *STRAT* CV37 .... **29** E3
Makepeace Av *WWCK* CV34 ...... **2** B1
Malham Rd *WWCK* CV34 .... **2** C1 🔲
The Malins *WWCK* CV34 .... **3** H7
Mallard Cl *STRAT* CV37 .... **26** D2
Mallory Dr *WWCK* CV34 .... **16** B3
The Maltings *RLSN* CV32 .... **12** B5
Mander Gv *WWCK* CV34 .... **20** D1
Manor Dr *STRAT* CV37 .... **24** D4
Manor Gn *STRAT* CV37 .... **7** K5
Manor Rd *RLSN* CV32 .... **12** D4
...*STRAT* CV37 .... **7** J5
Mansell St *STRAT* CV37 .... **6** D3
Manston Dr *RWWCK/WEL* CV35 .. **31** F5
Maple Gv *STRAT* CV37 .... **27** G2
...*WWCK* CV34 .... **3** F1
Maple Rd *RLSS* CV31 .... **5** F7
Marcroft Pl *RLSS* CV31 .... **19** F4
Mark Antony Dr *WWCK* CV34 .... **22** D1
Market Pl *WWCK* CV34 .... **2** A6
Market St *WWCK* CV34 .... **16** B4 🔲
Markham Dr *RLSS* CV31 .... **23** H2
Marlborough Dr *RLSS* CV31 ..... **19** E4
Marloes Wk *RLSS* CV31 .... **19** E4
Marsham Cl *WWCK* CV34 .... **3** H2
Marsh Rd *STRAT* CV37 .... **24** B3
Marston Cl *RLSN* CV32 .... **12** C4
Marten Cl *RWWCK/WEL* CV35 .... **15** G3 🔲
Martin Cl *STRAT* CV37 .... **27** H2
Masefield Av *WWCK* CV34 .... **21** E1
Masefield Rd *STRAT* CV37 .... **7** H7

Mason Av *RLSN* CV32 .... **13** E4
Masons Rd *STRAT* CV37 .... **27** E3
Masons Wy *STRAT* CV37 .... **27** E3 🔲
Masters Rd *RLSS* CV31 .... **23** G1
Mathe Cft *RLSS* CV31 .... **19** E5
Matthews Cl *STRAT* CV37 .... **27** H3 🔲
Maybrook Rd *STRAT* CV37 .... **6** C1
Mayfield Av *STRAT* CV37 .... **6** E1
Mayfield Ct *STRAT* CV37 .... **6** E1
Maynard Av *WWCK* CV34 .... **3** F4
Mayne Cl *RWWCK/WEL* CV35 .... **15** F4
Meadow Cl *RLSN* CV32 .... **13** E3
...*STRAT* CV37 .... **27** E4
Meadow Lea *STRAT* CV37 .... **27** E4
Meadow Sweet Rd *STRAT* CV37 .. **27** E2
Medley Gv *RLSS* CV31 .... **23** F2
Meer St *STRAT* CV37 .... **6** E3
Melton Rd *RLSN* CV32 .... **12** C5
Mercia Wy *WWCK* CV34 .... **3** F5
Mews Rd *RLSN* CV32 .... **4** B2
Mickleton Dr *RWWCK/WEL* CV35.. **8** D5
Middle Lock La *RWWCK/WEL* CV35.. **8** D5
Mildmay Cl *STRAT* CV37 .... **33** E1 🔲
Milestone Dr *STRAT* CV37 .... **34** D2
Millbank *WWCK* CV34 .... **17** E1 🔲
Millers Rd *WWCK* CV34 .... **16** B2
Mill House Cl *WWCK* CV34 .... **3** J3
Mill House Dr *WWCK* CV34 ...... **3** J3
Mill House Ter *RLSN* CV32 .... **4** B2
Mill La *RLSN* CV32 .... **13** H2
...*STRAT* CV37 .... **6** E6
Mill Rd *RLSS* CV31 .... **5** G3
Mill St *RLSN* CV32 .... **5** G4
...*WWCK* CV34 .... **2** C6
Milton Av *WWCK* CV34 .... **16** A5 🔲
Milverton Crs West *RLSN* CV32 .. **18** A1 🔲
Milverton Hl *RLSN* CV32 .... **4** C2
Milverton Lawn *RLSN* CV32 ..... **4** B2 🔲
Milverton Ter *RLSN* CV32 .... **4** C2
Minster Cl *RWWCK/WEL* CV35 .. **15** F4 🔲
Moat Gn *RWWCK/WEL* CV35..... **20** C4
Mollington Rd *RLSS* CV31 .... **23** G2
Monarch's Wy *STRAT* CV37 ...... **27** H2
Monks Wy *WWCK* CV34 .... **16** B4 🔲
Montague Rd *WWCK* CV34........ **2** E1
Montcrieff Dr *RLSS* CV31 .... **19** E5
Montgomery Av
...*RWWCK/WEL* CV35 .... **15** E4 🔲
Montgomery Cl *STRAT* CV37 .... **6** A6
Montrose Av *RLSN* CV32 .... **12** C3
Monument Wy *STRAT* CV37 ..... **27** H2 🔲
Moore Cl *WWCK* CV34 .... **10** C5 🔲
Moorhill Rd *RLSS* CV31 .... **23** G2
Mordaunt Rd *RWWCK/WEL* CV35.. **31** H3
Moreton Cl *STRAT* CV37 .... **28** C5 🔲
Morrell St *RLSN* CV32 .... **18** B1
Morris Dr *RLSS* CV31 .... **23** G2
Morse Rd *RLSS* CV31 .... **23** G3
Morton St *RLSN* CV32 .... **18** B1
Mosspaul Cl *RLSN* CV32 .... **11** H5
Moss St *RLSS* CV31 .... **5** G5 🔲
Mountbatten Cl *STRAT* CV37 .... **33** E1
Mount Crs *STRAT* CV37 .... **26** D4
Mountford Cl *RWWCK/WEL* CV35.. **31** H4
Mount Pleasant *STRAT* CV37 ... **26** D4 🔲
Mulberry Cl *RLSN* CV32 .... **12** C5
Mulberry St *STRAT* CV37 .... **6** E2
Mullard Dr *RLSS* CV31 .... **23** G2
Murcott Rd East *RLSS* CV31 ..... **23** G2
Murcott Rd West *RLSS* CV31 .... **23** G2
Myton Crs *WWCK* CV34 .... **3** H6
Myton Crofts *RLSS* CV31 .... **4** A5
Myton Gdns *WWCK* CV34 .... **3** F6
Myton La *WWCK* CV34............... **3** H6
Myton Rd *WWCK* CV34 .... **2** E7

N

Napton Dr *RLSN* CV32 .... **12** C5
Narrow La *STRAT* CV37 .... **6** D5
The Nashes *STRAT* CV37 .... **33** F5
Neilston St *RLSS* CV31 .... **5** G5 🔲
Nelson Av *WWCK* CV34 .... **3** F1
Nelson La *WWCK* CV34 .... **2** D2
Nevill Cl *RLSS* CV31 .... **4** E7
Neville Gv *WWCK* CV34 .... **2** D1
Newbold Pl *RLSN* CV32 .... **5** G2
...*RWWCK/WEL* CV35 .... **31** H3
Newbold St *RLSN* CV32 .... **5** G2
Newbold Ter *RLSN* CV32 .... **5** G3
Newbold Ter East *RLSN* CV32 ... **5** H2
New Broad St *STRAT* CV37 .... **6** C6
New Brook St *RLSN* CV32 .... **4** D2
Newburgh Crs *WWCK* CV34 ...... **2** A2
Newbury Cl *RLSS* CV31 .... **19** E4 🔲

New Cl *RWWCK/WEL* CV35 .... **15** F4 🔲
Newdigate *RLSS* CV31 .... **19** E5
Newland Rd *RLSN* CV32 .... **13** E4
Newmarket Cl *STRAT* CV37 ...... **6** A7
...*STRAT* CV37 .... **33** F2 🔲
Newnham Rd *RLSN* CV32 .... **12** D4
Newsholme Cl *WWCK* CV34 ...... **16** C1 🔲
New St *RLSN* CV32 .... **13** G2
...*RLSS* CV31 .... **5** G4
...*STRAT* CV37 .... **6** D7
...*STRAT* CV37 .... **28** D3
...*WWCK* CV34 .... **2** A6 🔲
Nicholson Cl *WWCK* CV34 .... **16** D1 🔲
Noble Cl *WWCK* CV34 .... **16** B5
Norfolk St *RLSN* CV32 .... **18** C1
Normanby Mdw *RLSS* CV31 ..... **23** G3
Normandy Cl
...*RWWCK/WEL* CV35 .... **15** G3 🔲
North Cl *RLSN* CV32 .... **13** G2
Northcote St *RLSS* CV31 .... **5** K4
Northgate St *WWCK* CV34 .... **2** A5 🔲
Northumberland Rd *RLSN* CV32.. **12** A5
North Villiers St *RLSN* CV32 ..... **18** C1
Northway *RLSS* CV31 .... **5** H7
Norton Dr *WWCK* CV34 .... **10** B5
Nursery La *RLSS* CV31 .... **18** C5

O

Oak Ct *WWCK* CV34 .... **23** E3
Oakleigh Rd *STRAT* CV37 .... **27** F2
Oakridge Rd *RLSN* CV32 .... **13** E3
Oak Rd *STRAT* CV37 .... **28** D4
Oak Tree Cl *RLSN* CV32 .... **12** C5
Oakwood Gv *WWCK* CV34 .... **17** E1
Oberon Cl *WWCK* CV34 .... **23** E1 🔲
Offchurch La *RLSS* CV31 .... **19** H4
Offchurch Rd *RLSN* CV32 .... **13** G3
Oken Rd *WWCK* CV34 .... **16** B2 🔲
Old Budbrooke Rd
...*RWWCK/WEL* CV35 .... **15** F4
Old Mill Br *WWCK* CV34 .... **2** C7
Old Milverton La *RLSN* CV32 .... **12** A3
Old Milverton Rd *RLSN* CV32 ... **11** G4
Old School La *RWWCK/WEL* CV35 .. **20** A1
...*STRAT* CV37 .... **24** D4
Old School Ms *RLSN* CV32 ...... **12** D4 🔲
Old Sq *WWCK* CV34 .... **2** A6
Old Town *STRAT* CV37 .... **6** D5
Old Town Ms *STRAT* CV37 .... **6** C7
Old Warwick Rd *RLSS* CV31 ..... **4** D5
Olympus Av *RLSN* CV32 .... **4** A7
Onslow Cft *RLSN* CV32 .... **12** B5
Ophelia Dr *WWCK* CV34 .... **23** E1
Orchard Wy *STRAT* CV37.......... **6** B5
Orford Cl *RWWCK/WEL* CV35 .... **31** H4 🔲
Orrian Cl *STRAT* CV37 .... **27** F2
Osborne Ct *RLSS* CV31 .... **23** G1 🔲
Oswald Rd *RLSN* CV32 .... **4** B1
Othello Av *WWCK* CV34............ **23** F3
Overell Gv *RLSN* CV32 .... **11** G5
Overtons Cl *RLSN* CV32 .... **19** H5 🔲
Oxford Pl *RLSN* CV32 .... **5** F1
Oxford Rw *RLSN* CV32 .... **5** F1
Oxford St *RLSN* CV32 .... **18** B1

P

Packington Pl *RLSS* CV31 .... **5** G5 🔲
Packmore St *WWCK* CV34 .... **2** C3
Packwood Cl *RLSS* CV31........... **19** E5
Paddock La *STRAT* CV37 .... **6** A7
The Paddocks *WWCK* CV34 ...... **2** C5
Palmer Rd *RLSS* CV31 .... **23** H1
Pampas Cl *STRAT* CV37 .... **27** F2
Parade *RLSN* CV32 .... **5** F1
Paradise St *WWCK* CV34 .... **2** C3
Park Ct *STRAT* CV37 .... **6** B1
Park Dr *RLSS* CV31 .... **4** C4
Parkes St *WWCK* CV34 .... **16** B3
Parklands Av *RLSN* CV32 .... **13** E3
Park Rd *RLSN* CV32 .... **12** B3
Park St *RLSN* CV32 .... **5** F1
Parr Cl *RLSS* CV31 .... **3** A6
Partridge Rd *STRAT* CV37 .... **26** D3 🔲
Pattens Rd *WWCK* CV34 .... **17** F1
Payne Cl *RLSN* CV32 .... **12** C5
Payton St *STRAT* CV37 .... **6** E3
Peacock Cl *RWWCK/WEL* CV35 .. **31** G4 🔲
The Peacocks *WWCK* CV34 ...... **20** D5
Peel Rd *WWCK* CV34 .... **2** A2
Pembroke Cl *WWCK* CV34 .... **2** C2
Penfold Cl *BTACH/HAR* CV33 ... **22** D5
Penns Cl *RLSN* CV32 .... **13** G2

Pennystone Cl *RLSS* CV31 .... 19 F4
Penrith Cl *RLSN* CV32 .... 11 G5
Percy Rd *WWCK* CV34 .... 2 A2
Percy St *STRAT* CV37 .... 6 E1
Percy Ter *RLSN* CV32 .... 4 B1
Pheasant Cl *STRAT* CV37 .... 26 D3 ☒
Phillippes Rd *WWCK* CV34 .... 2 D1
Pickard St *WWCK* CV34 .... 2 E4
Piers Cl *WWCK* CV34 .... 2 D2
Pimlico La *STRAT* CV37 .... 29 E5
Pine Cl *STRAT* CV37 .... 33 E1
Pinehurst *RLSN* CV32 .... 13 G2
Pleasant Wy *RLSN* CV32 .... 12 C5
Plover Cl *STRAT* CV37 .... 26 D2
Plymouth Pl *RLSS* CV31 .... 5 H4
Portland House *RLSN* CV32 .... 4 E2
Portland Ms *RLSN* CV32 .... 4 E2 ☒
Portland Pl *RLSN* CV32 .... 4 D2
Portland Pl West *RLSN* CV32 .... 4 D2
Portland St *RLSN* CV32 .... 4 E2
Portway Cl *RLSS* CV31 .... 19 F4
Pound La *RLSN* CV32 .... 12 C4
Powers Cl *RLSN* CV32 .... 4 E1
Price Rd *RLSN* CV32 .... 13 G2
Primrose Hl *WWCK* CV34 .... 10 B5
Prince's Dr *RLSN* CV32 .... 4 A3
      RLSS CV31 .... 4 B4
Prince's St *RLSN* CV32 .... 18 D1
Priory Ms *WWCK* CV34 .... 2 A5
Priory Rd *WWCK* CV34 .... 2 B5
Priory St *RLSS* CV31 .... 5 F6
Priory Ter *RLSS* CV31 .... 5 F6
Prospect Rd *RLSS* CV31 .... 18 D5
Purser Dr *WWCK* CV31 .... 20 D1
Purton Ms *RLSS* CV31 .... 19 E4

Q

Quail Cl *STRAT* CV37 .... 26 D3
Quarry St *RLSN* CV32 .... 3 K1
Queen's Sq *WWCK* CV34 .... 16 B5 ☒
Queen St *RLSN* CV32 .... 13 F2
      RLSN CV32 .... 4 A1
Queensway *RLSS* CV31 .... 4 C6
      RLSS CV31 .... 18 B5
Quiney's Cl *STRAT* CV37 .... 33 E1

R

Radbrook Wy *RLSS* CV31 .... 19 F4 ☒
Radford Rd *RLSS* CV31 .... 5 H5
Rainsford Cl *STRAT* CV37 .... 33 G5
Ramsey Rd *RLSS* CV31 .... 5 K5
Randolph Cl *RLSN* CV31 .... 19 E4 ☒
Ranelagh St *RLSS* CV31 .... 5 G6
Ranelagh Ter *RLSS* CV31 .... 5 F6
Range Meadow Cl *RLSN* CV32 .... 11 G4
Ravensdale Av *RLSN* CV32 ...... 11 G5 ☒
Rawlinson Rd *RLSN* CV32 .... 12 D5 ☒
Reardon Ct *WWCK* CV34 .... 16 C1 ☒☒
Rectory Cl *RLSS* CV31 .... 23 H1
Redcar Cl *RLSN* CV32 .... 12 D3
Redland Rd *RLSS* CV31 .... 18 D5
Redlands Crs *STRAT* CV37 .... 26 D4
Redwing Cl *STRAT* CV37 .... 26 D2
Regal Rd *STRAT* CV37 .... 6 D1
Regent Gv *RLSN* CV32 .... 5 F2
Regent Pl *RLSN* CV32 .... 5 F4
Regent St *RLSN* CV32 .... 4 D2
Regnier Pl *WWCK* CV34 .... 23 F3
Remburn Gdns *WWCK* CV34 .... 2 C3
Richards Gv *RLSS* CV31 .... 18 C5
Richardson Cl *WWCK* CV34 ... 16 D1 ☒☒
Rich Cl *WWCK* CV34 .... 3 F4
Ridgeley Cl *WWCK* CV34 .... 10 B5
The Ridgeway *WWCK* CV34 .... 2 E1
Ridgewood Cl *RLSN* CV32 .... 17 G1
The Ridgway *STRAT* CV37 .... 26 C3
Rigby Cl *WWCK* CV34 .... 22 D1
Risdale Cl *RLSN* CV32 .... 11 G5
River Cl *RLSN* CV32 .... 4 A3
Rivermead Dr *STRAT* CV37 .... 28 D3 ☒
Robins Gv *WWCK* CV34 .... 21 E1 ☒
Rock Mill La *RLSN* CV32 .... 3 J1
Roe Cl *WWCK* CV34 .... 2 C3
Rogers Wy *WWCK* CV34 .... 20 D1 ☒
Romeo Arbour *WWCK* CV34 ..... 23 E2
Rosefield Pl *RLSN* CV32 .... 5 F3
Rosefield St *RLSN* CV32 .... 5 G2
Rosewood Crs *RLSN* CV32 .... 12 D5
Rotherfield Cl *RLSS* CV31 .... 5 J4
Rother St *STRAT* CV37 .... 6 D3 ☒
Rothwell Rd *WWCK* CV34 .... 16 A1
Rowan Cl *STRAT* CV37 .... 27 G2 ☒

Rowan Dr *WWCK* CV34 .... 2 D2
Rowborough Cl
      RWWCK/WEL CV35 .... 9 E5 ☒
Rowley Crs *STRAT* CV37 .... 7 F1
Rowley Rd *RLSS* CV31 .... 23 G3
Roxburgh Cft *RLSN* CV32 .... 12 D2
Rugby Rd *BTACH/HAR* CV33 .... 13 H1
      RLSN CV32 .... 3 K2
Rushbrook Rd *STRAT* CV37 .... 7 J7
Rushmore St *RLSS* CV31 .... 5 J5
Russell St *RLSN* CV32 .... 4 E1
Russell Ter *RLSS* CV31 .... 5 H4
Ryder Cl *RWWCK/WEL* CV35 ... 15 F4 ☒
Rye Cl *STRAT* CV37 .... 27 F2 ☒
Ryland Cl *RLSS* CV31 .... 5 K7
Ryland St *RLSN* CV32 .... 6 D6

S

Sackville Cl *STRAT* CV37 .... 26 D3
Sadler Cl *STRAT* CV37 .... 27 G1 ☒
Saffron Meadow *STRAT* CV37 ...... 6 D7
Saffron Wk *STRAT* CV37 .... 6 D7
St Albans Cl *RLSN* CV32 .... 11 G5 ☒
St Andrew's Crs *STRAT* CV37 ... 6 B4 ☒
St Andrew's Rd *RLSN* CV32 ...... 12 D2
Saintbury Cl *STRAT* CV37 ...... 34 C1 ☒
St Catherine's Crs *RLSS* CV31... 23 F2
St Christopher's Cl
      WWCK CV34 .... 16 B2 ☒
St George's Cl *STRAT* CV37 .... 27 E3 ☒
St George's Rd *RLSS* CV31 .... 5 F7
St Gregory's Rd *STRAT* CV37 ...... 7 F2
St Helen's Rd *RLSN* CV32 .... 18 B5
St James' Av
      RWWCK/WEL CV35 .... 31 G3 ☒
St James Meadow Rd *RLSN* CV32 .. 17 G1
St Johns *WWCK* CV34 .... 2 C5
St Johns Cl *STRAT* CV37 .... 6 C6
St John's Rd *RLSS* CV31 .... 5 G7
St Laurence Av *WWCK* CV34 .... 16 B5
St Margaret's Rd *RLSS* CV31 .... 18 C5
St Mark's Ms *RLSN* CV32 .... 18 A1 ☒
St Mark's Rd *RLSN* CV32 .... 17 H1
St Martin's Cl *STRAT* CV37 .... 6 B4
St Mary's Cl *WWCK* CV34 ...... 16 B2 ☒
St Mary's Crs *RLSS* CV31 .... 5 J5
St Mary's Rd *RLSS* CV31 .... 5 J4
      STRAT CV37 .... 6 E1
St Mary's Ter *RLSS* CV31 .... 5 J5
St Michael's Rd *WWCK* CV34 .... 16 B2
St Nicholas Church St *WWCK* CV34 .. 2 C6
St Peter's Rd *RLSN* CV32 .... 4 E3 ☒
      RWWCK/WEL CV35 .... 31 G3
Saltisford *WWCK* CV34 .... 2 A5
Saltisford Gdns *WWCK* CV34 ... 16 B2 ☒
Sanctus Dr *STRAT* CV37 .... 6 C6
Sanctus Rd *STRAT* CV37 .... 6 C6
Sanctus St *STRAT* CV37 .... 6 D6
Sandel Cl *STRAT* CV37 .... 6 A2
Sandfield Rd *STRAT* CV37 .... 6 C7
Sandown Cl *RLSN* CV32 .... 13 E3
Sandpiper St *STRAT* CV37 .... 27 E2
Sandy La *RLSN* CV32 .... 11 G4
      RLSN CV32 .... 12 B2
Sapphire Dr *RLSS* CV31 .... 18 B5 ☒
Sargeaunt St *RLSS* CV31 .... 4 E5
Satchwell Ct *RLSN* CV32 .... 5 F2
Satchwell St *RLSN* CV32 .... 5 F1
Saumur Wy *RLSS* CV31 .... 3 K6
      WWCK CV34 .... 3 K6
Saxon Cl *STRAT* CV37 .... 7 H4
Scar Bank *WWCK* CV34 .... 2 A1
Scholars La *STRAT* CV37 .... 6 D5
School La *RLSS* CV31 .... 19 G5
      STRAT CV37 .... 28 D2
School Rd *RWWCK/WEL* CV35 .. 31 G4
Scott Rd *RLSS* CV31 .... 5 J7
The Seekings *RLSS* CV31 .... 23 H2
Selwyn Cl *RWWCK/WEL* CV35 .. 31 G3
Semele Cl *RLSS* CV31 .... 19 G5
Seven Meadows Rd *STRAT* CV37 .. 6 D7
      STRAT CV37 .... 33 H2
Severn Cl *STRAT* CV37 .... 13 E4
Sevincott Cl *STRAT* CV37 .... 26 D3
Seymour Cl
      RWWCK/WEL CV35 .... 15 F4 ☒☒
Seymour Gv *RLSN* CV32 .... 4 A6
Seymour Rd *STRAT* CV37 .... 33 E1
Shakespeare Av *WWCK* CV34 ... 21 E1 ☒
Shakespeare St *STRAT* CV37 ...... 6 E3
Sharpe Cl *WWCK* CV34 .... 3 F4
Sheepcote La *RLSN* CV32 ...... 18 C1 ☒
Sheep St *STRAT* CV37 .... 6 E4
Shelbourne Rd *STRAT* CV37 ..... 26 C3
Sheldon Gv *WWCK* CV34 ...... 10 D5 ☒

Shelley Av *WWCK* CV34 .... 21 E1
Shelley Rd *STRAT* CV37 .... 7 H7
Sherwood Wk *RLSN* CV32 .... 13 E3
Shipston Rd *STRAT* CV37 .... 7 G7
      STRAT CV37 .... 33 H3
Shottery *STRAT* CV37 .... 27 E5
Shottery Rd *STRAT* CV37 .... 6 A5
Shrubland St *RLSS* CV31 .... 5 H7
Shuckburgh Gv *RLSN* CV32 .... 12 C5 ☒
Sidelands Rd *STRAT* CV37 ...... 26 D4 ☒
Silver Birch Gv *RLSS* CV31 ..... 18 B5 ☒
Simmons Ct
      RWWCK/WEL CV35 .... 31 G4 ☒
Slade Hl *RWWCK/WEL* CV35 .. 15 F3 ☒
Slade Meadow *RLSS* CV31 .... 19 G5
Slingates Rd *STRAT* CV37 .... 27 H3
Smith St *RLSS* CV31 .... 5 F4 ☒
      WWCK CV34 .... 2 C5
Smythe Gv *WWCK* CV34 .... 2 B1
Somers Pl *RLSN* CV32 .... 4 D2
Southern La *STRAT* CV37 .... 6 E6
South Green Dr *STRAT* CV37 .... 26 D5
Southlands *RLSS* CV31 .... 5 J4
Southlea Av *RLSS* CV31 .... 4 D6
Southlea Cl *RLSS* CV31 .... 4 D6
South View Rd *RLSN* CV32 ...... 13 E2
Southway *RLSS* CV31 .... 18 C5
Spartan Cl *RLSS* CV31 .... 23 E1
Spa Vw *RLSS* CV31 .... 23 H1
Spencer Av *RLSN* CV32 .... 5 F4
Spencer St *RLSN* CV32 .... 5 F4
Spencer Yd *RLSN* CV32 .... 5 F4
Spilsbury Cl *RLSN* CV32 .... 12 A5
Spinney Hl *WWCK* CV32 .... 2 E1
The Spinney *RLSN* CV32 .... 4 A1
Spring La *RLSS* CV31 .... 19 G5
Spring Pool *WWCK* CV34 .... 2 A4
Springwell Rd *RLSS* CV31 ..... 19 F4 ☒
Spruce Gv *RLSS* CV31 .... 18 B5 ☒
Standlake Ms *RLSS* CV31 ...... 19 E4 ☒
Stand St *WWCK* CV34 .... 16 B4 ☒
Stannells Cl *STRAT* CV37 .... 32 D2
Stanton Rd *RLSS* CV31 .... 19 E4
Station Ap *RLSS* CV31 .... 4 E4
Station Av *WWCK* CV34 .... 2 D4
Station Rd *STRAT* CV37 .... 6 C5
      STRAT CV37 .... 25 E3
      WWCK CV34 .... 2 C4
Staunton Rd *RLSS* CV31 .... 18 C5
Stidfall Gv *RLSS* CV31 .... 19 F4
Stirling Av *RLSN* CV32 .... 12 D2
Stockton Gv *RLSN* CV32 .... 12 C5 ☒
Stonehouse Cl *RLSN* CV32 ...... 12 A5
Stoneleigh Rd *RLSN* CV32 .... 12 B1
Stone Pits *STRAT* CV37 .... 24 C3
Stone Pits Meadow
      STRAT CV37 .... 24 C3 ☒
Strachey Av *RLSN* CV32 .... 12 A5
Stratford Rd *RWWCK/WEL* CV35... 20 A5
      WWCK CV34 .... 21 E2
      WWCK CV34 .... 21 F1 ☒
Strathearn Rd *RLSN* CV32 .... 18 A1
Stretton Crs *RLSS* CV31 .... 23 H1
Stuart Cl *WWCK* CV34 .... 16 B5 ☒
Stuart Ct *RLSN* CV32 .... 4 D1 ☒
Styles Cl *RLSS* CV31 .... 5 H5
Sudbury Cl *RLSN* CV32 .... 13 E5
Suffolk St *RLSN* CV32 .... 18 C1
Summerton Rd *RLSS* CV31 ...... 23 G2
Sumner Cl *RWWCK/WEL* CV35 ... 15 F4 ☒
Sutherland Cl *WWCK* CV34 ... 16 C1 ☒☒
Swadling St *RLSN* CV32 .... 4 E6
Swain Crofts *RLSS* CV31 .... 5 K7
Swallow Cl *STRAT* CV37 .... 27 H2
Swanfold *STRAT* CV37 .... 24 D4
Swans Cl *STRAT* CV37 .... 24 D5
Swan's Nest *STRAT* CV37 .... 7 G5
Swan St *RLSN* CV32 .... 5 G1
      WWCK CV34 .... 2 A6
Swift Rd *STRAT* CV37 .... 27 H2
Sycamore Cl *RWWCK/WEL* CV35 ... 31 H4
      STRAT CV37 .... 27 H2 ☒
Sycamore Gv *WWCK* CV34 ..... 17 E1 ☒
Sydenham Dr *RLSN* CV32 .... 5 K7

T

Tachbrook Park Dr *RLSS* CV31 .... 4 B6 ☒
Tachbrook Rd *RLSS* CV31 .... 5 F6
      RLSS CV31 .... 18 B5
Tachbrook St *RLSS* CV31 .... 5 H7
      RLSS CV31 .... 18 B5
Talbot Rd *STRAT* CV37 .... 27 H3
Tavern La *STRAT* CV37 .... 27 E5
Tavistock St *RLSN* CV32 .... 4 E1
Taylor Av *RLSN* CV32 .... 12 D5

Teal Cl *STRAT* CV37 26
Telford Av *RLSN* CV32 12
The Templars *WWCK* CV34 16
Temple Gv *WWCK* CV34.............. 16
Tennyson Av *RLSN* CV32 .... 21 E☒
Tennyson Rd *STRAT* CV37 34
Terry Av *RLSN* CV32 17
Theatre St *WWCK* CV34 .... 16 B☒
Thomas St *RLSN* CV32 5
Thornley Cl *RLSS* CV31 19
Thorn Stile Cl *RLSN* CV32 13
Thornton Cl *WWCK* CV34 .... 2 C☒
Three Cornered Cl *RLSN* CV32 13
Thursfield Rd *RLSN* CV32 .... 12 D4
Tiddington Flds *STRAT* CV37 ..... 28 ☒
Tiddington Rd *STRAT* CV37 .... 28 ☒
Tidmington Cl
      RWWCK/WEL CV35 .... 9 E☒
Timothy's Bridge Rd *STRAT* CV37 .. 27
Tink-a-tank *WWCK* CV34 .... 2 B5
Tithe Barn Cl
      RWWCK/WEL CV35 .... 15 F☒
Toll Gate Cl *STRAT* CV37 .... 26 ☒
Touchstone Rd *WWCK* CV34 .. 23 E☒
Tower Cl *STRAT* CV37 27
Townesend Cl *WWCK* CV34 .... 2 ☒
Townsend Rd *STRAT* CV37 28
Tressel Cft *WWCK* CV34............. 23
Trevelyan Crs *STRAT* CV37 .... 26 ☒
Trinity St *RLSN* CV32 18
      STRAT CV37 .... 6 ☒
Troutbeck Av *RLSN* CV32 11
Trueman Cl *WWCK* CV34 .... 2 ☒
Tudor Ct *WWCK* CV34 .... 16 B5
Turner Cl *STRAT* CV37 .... 20 ☒
Turpin Ct *RLSS* CV31 .... 4 ☒
Tybalt Cl *WWCK* CV34 .... 22 ☒
Tyler St *STRAT* CV37 .... 6 E3☒

U

Ullswater Av *RLSN* CV32 .... 11 ☒
Union Rd *RLSN* CV32 .... 4 ☒
Union St *STRAT* CV37 .... 6 ☒
Upper Grove St *RLSN* CV32 .... 4 ☒
Upper Holly Wk *RLSN* CV32 .... 5 ☒

V

Valentine Cl *STRAT* CV37 .... 33 F2
Valletta Wy *RWWCK/WEL* CV35 .. 31 ☒
Valley Rd *RLSN* CV32 .... 12 ☒
Verden Av *WWCK* CV34 .... 20 ☒
Verdun Cl *RLSS* CV31 .... 23 ☒
Vermont Gv *RLSS* CV31 .... 19 ☒
Verney Dr *STRAT* CV37 .... 27 ☒
Verney Gdns *STRAT* CV37 .... 27 ☒
Vernon Cl *RLSN* CV32 .... 12 ☒
Vicarage Fld *WWCK* CV34 .... 3 ☒
Vicarage La *RWWCK/WEL* CV35 .. 20 ☒
Vicarage Rd *RLSN* CV32 .... 12 ☒
Victoria St *RLSS* CV31 .... 4 ☒
      WWCK CV34 .... 16 ☒
Victoria Ter *RLSS* CV31 .... 5 ☒
Villebon Wy *RLSS* CV31 .... 23 ☒
Villiers St *RLSN* CV32 .... 18 ☒
Vincent Av *STRAT* CV37............ 27 ☒
Vincent St *RLSN* CV32 .... 5 ☒
      RLSN CV32 .... 18 ☒
Vine La *WWCK* CV34 .... 2 ☒
Viscount Cl *RLSS* CV31 .... 4 ☒

W

Wackrill Dr *RLSN* CV32 .... 13 ☒
Wade Gv *WWCK* CV34 .... 10 ☒
Wake Gv *WWCK* CV34 .... 15 H5
Walford Gv *WWCK* CV34 .... 16 ☒
Walkers Rd *STRAT* CV37 .... 27 ☒
Waller St *RLSN* CV32 .... 12 ☒
Wallsgrove Cl *RLSN* CV32 .... 12 ☒
Walnut Dr *STRAT* CV37 .... 12 ☒
Walton Rd *RWWCK/WEL* CV35... 31 ☒
Walton Wy *RWWCK/WEL* CV35 .. 31 ☒
Ward Gv *WWCK* CV34 .... 3 ☒
Warmington Gv *WWCK* CV34 .. 15 H2☒
Warner Cl *WWCK* CV34 .... 16 B1☒
Warren Cl *RLSN* CV32 .... 12 ☒
Warwick By-pass
      RWWCK/WEL CV35 .... 20 ☒
Warwick Crs *STRAT* CV37 .... 7 C☒
Warwick New Rd *RLSN* CV32 .... 3 K☒

arwick Pl *RLSN* CV32 .... 4 C1
arwick Rd *RWWCK/WEL* CV35 ... 11 E2
  RWWCK/WEL CV35 .... 31 G2
  STRAT CV37 .... 7 F3
  STRAT CV37 .... 28 B3
arwick St *RLSN* CV32 .... 4 E1
asdale Cl *RLSN* CV32 .... 11 C5
ashbourne Rd *RLSS* CV31 ...... 23 G2
aterloo Cl
  RWWCK/WEL CV35 .... 31 F5
aterloo Ct *WWCK* CV34 .... 3 F3
aterloo Dr *STRAT* CV37 .... 34 C1
aterloo Pl *RLSN* CV32 .... 4 D1
aterloo St *RLSS* CV31 .... 5 K5
aterside *STRAT* CV37 .... 7 F4
atery La *RWWCK/WEL* CV35 .... 20 C4
athen Rd *RLSN* CV32 .... 12 C5
  WWCK CV34 .... 2 B2
atson Cl *WWCK* CV34 .... 2 B1
averley Rd *RLSS* CV31 .... 5 J7
averton Ms *RLSS* CV31 .... 19 E4
avytree Cl *WWCK* CV34 .... 16 B3
eale Gv *WWCK* CV34 .... 10 D5
ednock Gn *WWCK* CV34 .... 16 B2
ednock La *HENAR* B95 .... 16 A1
eilerswist Dr *RLSS* CV31 .... 23 G1
elcombe Rd *STRAT* CV37 .... 7 F2
elford Gv *RWWCK/WEL* CV35 .... 8 D4
ellesbourne Gv *STRAT* CV37 ..... 6 C4
ellesbourne Rd *STRAT* CV37 .... 29 F2

Wellington Dr *STRAT* CV37 .... 34 C1
Wellington Rd *RLSN* CV32 .... 12 D4
Welsh Cl *WWCK* CV34 .... 10 C5
Welsh Rd *RLSN* CV32 .... 13 H4
Wentworth Rd *RLSS* CV31 .... 19 F4
Westcliff Dr *WWCK* CV34 .... 10 C5
Western Rd *STRAT* CV37 .... 6 C2
Westfield Cl *STRAT* CV37 .... 27 G2
Westfield Crs *RWWCK/WEL* CV35 .. 31 F4
Westgate Cl *WWCK* CV34 .... 16 B4
West Green Dr *STRAT* CV37 ..... 26 C4
Westhill Rd *RLSN* CV32 .... 12 C1
Westlea Rd *RLSS* CV31 .... 4 D6
Weston Cl *RLSS* CV31 .... 19 E4
  WWCK CV34 .... 2 D5
West St *RLSS* CV31 .... 5 C5
  STRAT CV37 .... 6 D6
  WWCK CV34 .... 16 B5
West View Rd *RLSN* CV32 .... 13 E2
Wharf Rd *STRAT* CV37 .... 6 C1
Wharf Rd *WWCK* CV34 .... 2 E3
The Wharf *STRAT* CV37 .... 25 E3
Wheathill Cl *RLSN* CV32 .... 12 A5
Whitacre Rd *RLSN* CV32 .... 12 C5
Whitehead Cl *RWWCK/WEL* CV35 .. 31 H3
Whitehorn Dr *RLSN* CV32 .... 12 D5
Whitfield Cl *STRAT* CV37 .... 28 D3
Whitmore Rd *RLSN* CV32 .... 23 G2
Whitnash Rd *RLSS* CV31 .... 23 H2
Whittington Cl *WWCK* CV34 ..... 3 G3
Whitworth Cl *RWWCK/WEL* CV35 .. 31 F5

Willes Rd *RLSN* CV32 .... 5 H2
  RLSS CV31 .... 5 J4
Willes Ter *RLSS* CV31 .... 5 J3
Willett Gdns
  RWWCK/WEL CV35 .... 31 G5
William St *RLSN* CV32 .... 5 G2
William Tarver Cl *WWCK* CV34 .. 2 E5
Willow Dr *RWWCK/WEL* CV35 .. 31 G4
Willows Dr North *STRAT* CV37 .. 6 B3
Willow Sheets Meadow
  RLSN CV32 .... 13 G1
The Willows *STRAT* CV37 .... 6 B5
Wilmcote La *HENAR* B95 .... 24 A2
Wilnecote Gv *RLSS* CV31 .... 18 D5
Wincott Cl *STRAT* CV37 .... 7 K6
Windermere Dr *RLSN* CV32 ..... 11 H5
Winderton Av
  RWWCK/WEL CV35 .... 8 D5
Windmill Hl *RLSN* CV32 .... 13 F2
Windmill Rd *RLSN* CV32 .... 18 B5
Windsor Pl *RLSN* CV32 .... 4 E1
Windsor St *RLSN* CV32 .... 4 E1
  STRAT CV37 .... 4 D3
Winslow Cl *RLSN* CV32 .... 3 K1
Winston Cl *STRAT* CV37 .... 33 E1
Wise Gv *WWCK* CV34 .... 10 C5
Wise St *RLSS* CV31 .... 5 F5
Wise Ter *RLSS* CV31 .... 5 F5
Woburn Cl *RLSS* CV31 .... 19 E4
Woodbine St *RLSN* CV32 .... 4 D2
Woodcote Rd *RLSN* CV32 .... 12 B4

  WWCK CV34 .... 2 C4
Woodcot Park Dr *STRAT* CV37 .... 24 C3
Woodhouse St *WWCK* CV34 ... 16 B4
Woodlands Rd *STRAT* CV37 ..... 27 G2
Woodloes Av North *WWCK* CV34 .. 10 C5
Woodloes Av South *WWCK* CV34 .. 2 B1
Woodloes La *RWWCK/WEL* CV35... 10 C4
  WWCK CV34 .... 10 D5
Woodman Ct *STRAT* CV37 ...... 6 D1
Wood St *RLSN* CV32 .... 5 G2
  STRAT CV37 .... 6 E4
Woodville Rd *WWCK* CV34 ...... 2 B3
Woodward Cl *RLSS* CV31 .... 23 G3
Woodway *RWWCK/WEL* CV35 ... 15 E3
Woodway Av *RWWCK/WEL* CV35 .. 15 F4
Wootton Cl *STRAT* CV37 .... 28 C5
Wootton Ct *RLSN* CV32 .... 12 B5
Wordsworth Av *WWCK* CV34 .... 16 A5
Wych Elm Dr *RLSS* CV31 .... 18 B5
Wye Cl *RLSN* CV32 .... 13 E4
Wyvern Cl *RWWCK/WEL* CV35 .. 31 F5

Y

Yardley Cl *WWCK* CV34 .... 10 D5
Yarranton Cl *STRAT* CV37 ..... 27 F2
Yeomanry Cl *WWCK* CV34 ..... 2 C5
York Rd *RLSS* CV31 .... 4 E3
Young Cl *WWCK* CV34 .... 15 H5

Index - featured places

Il Saints C of E Middle School
  WWCK CV34 .... 3 F1
Il Saints C of E (VA) Community
  Primary School
  RWWCK/WEL CV35 ...... 11 E2
veston C of E Junior
  & Infant School
  STRAT CV37 .... 28 D4
nn Hathaway's Cottage
  STRAT CV37 .... 26 D5
rnold Lodge School
  RLSN CV32 .... 12 B5
he Art Gallery
  WWCK CV34 .... 16 B5
venue Farm Industrial Estate
  STRAT CV37 .... 27 F3
venue Fields Industrial Estate
  STRAT CV37 .... 27 E3
ylesford School
  WWCK CV34 .... 21 E1
ard's Walk Shopping Mall
  STRAT CV37 .... 6 E3
ishopton Junior & Infant School
  STRAT CV37 .... 26 D3
oat Club
  STRAT CV37 .... 7 F4
owling Green
  STRAT CV37 .... 7 F5
riar Hill County First School
  RLSN CV32 .... 23 H2
ridge Field
  WWCK CV34 .... 2 D7
ridge House Medical Centre
  STRAT CV37 .... 6 C5
ridge Town County Junior
  & Infant School
  STRAT CV37 .... 7 H7
road Street Junior
  & Infant School
  STRAT CV37 .... 6 C5
rookhurst Primary School
  RLSN CV32 .... 17 H1
udbrooke Combined School
  RWWCK/WEL CV35 ...... 15 F4
udbrooke Industrial Estate
  WWCK CV34 .... 16 A2
udbrooke Medical Centre
  RWWCK/WEL CV35 ...... 15 F3
udbrooke Road
  Industrial Estate
  RWWCK/WEL CV35 ...... 15 H3
utterfly Farm & Jungle Safari
  STRAT CV37 .... 7 G5
ampion School
  RLSS CV31 .... 19 E5

Cape Industrial Estate
  WWCK CV34 .... 2 A4
Cashmore Middle School
  RLSS CV31 .... 4 E7
Castle Gallery
  STRAT CV37 .... 6 E3
Civic Hall Theatre
  STRAT CV37 .... 6 D4
Clapham Terrace County
  First School
  RLSS CV31 .... 5 J5
Clubhouse
  STRAT CV37 .... 7 K3
Cricket Club
  WWCK CV34 .... 16 B5
Croft Medical Centre
  RLSS CV31 .... 19 E5
Cubbington C E
  Combined School
  RLSN CV32 .... 13 H2
Dene Park Industrial Estate
  RWWCK/WEL CV35 ...... 31 E4
The Dentists Surgery
  WWCK CV34 .... 16 C1
Emscote County First School
  WWCK CV34 .... 3 G3
Emscote Lawn
  Preparatory School
  STRAT CV37 .... 3 F3
The Ferncumbe C E C
  Primary School
  RWWCK/WEL CV35 ...... 8 A4
Golf Club Leisure Centre
  RLSN CV32 .... 5 K1
Grammar School & Guildhall
  STRAT CV37 .... 6 E5
Halls Croft Gallery
  STRAT CV37 .... 6 E5
Harvard House
  STRAT CV37 .... 6 E4
Haseley Business Centre
  RWWCK/WEL CV35 ...... 8 B2
Heathcote Hospital
  RLSS CV31 .... 23 F2
Heritage Theatre
  STRAT CV37 .... 6 E5
Hollywalk Clinic
  RLSN CV32 .... 5 G2
John Taylor Gallery
  WWCK CV34 .... 2 A7
Judith Shakespeare House
  STRAT CV37 .... 6 E4
Kings High School for Girls
  WWCK CV34 .... 2 B5

Kingsley School
  RLSN CV32 .... 18 B1
The Knibbs Shopping Centre
  WWCK CV34 .... 2 B5
The Lambert School
  STRAT CV37 .... 27 H2
Leamington Cricket Club
  RLSN CV32 .... 12 B5
Leamington Museum
  & Art Gallery
  RLSN CV32 .... 5 F3
Lillington Middle School
  RLSN CV32 .... 12 D4
Lillington Primary School
  RLSN CV32 .... 12 D4
Lisle Court Medical Centre
  RLSS CV31 .... 5 G6
Lisle Court Surgery
  RLSS CV31 .... 18 C5
The Loft Theatre
  RLSS CV31 .... 5 F4
Loquens Gallery
  STRAT CV37 .... 6 D3
Lord Leycester's Hospital
  WWCK CV34 .... 2 A6
Lowes Lane Industrial Estate
  RWWCK/WEL CV35 ...... 31 G5
Marie Corelli School
  STRAT CV37 .... 26 D3
Market
  STRAT CV37 .... 6 D3
Market Hall & Museum
  WWCK CV34 .... 2 A6
Mary Ardens House Museum
  STRAT CV37 .... 24 D3
Maybrook Industrial Estate
  STRAT CV37 .... 27 G3
Mid Warwickshire Gresham Day
  Special School
  RLSN CV32 .... 12 C4
Mid Warwickshire Magistrates
  RLSN CV32 .... 5 F3
Milverton Combined School
  RLSN CV32 .... 12 A5
The Minories Shopping Mall
  STRAT CV37 .... 6 E3
Montpellier Gallery
  STRAT CV37 .... 6 D4
Myton School
  WWCK CV34 .... 3 G6
Neil Astill Gallery
  WWCK CV34 .... 16 B4
Neilston Street Business Centre
  RLSS CV31 .... 5 H5

Newburgh Middle School
  WWCK CV34 .... 21 E1
New Place & Nash's House
  STRAT CV37 .... 6 E4
North Leamington School
  RLSN CV32 .... 12 B3
Nunhold Business Centre
  RWWCK/WEL CV35 ...... 14 A2
Old Warwickian Sports Ground
  RWWCK/WEL CV35 ...... 15 G5
The Other Place Theatre
  STRAT CV37 .... 6 E5
Our Lady & St Teresas R C
  Combined School
  RLSN CV32 .... 13 F2
Park St Surgery
  RLSN CV32 .... 5 F2
Playbox Theatre
  WWCK CV34 .... 21 E1
The Priory
  (County Record Office)
  WWCK CV34 .... 2 B4
Putting Green
  STRAT CV37 .... 7 F6
Queensway Trading Estate
  RLSS CV31 .... 4 D7
Racing Club Warwick FC
  WWCK CV34 .... 16 A5
Radford Semele C of E Combined
  School
  RLSS CV31 .... 19 G5
Red Lion Shopping Court
  STRAT CV37 .... 6 E4
Regency Business Centre
  RLSN CV32 .... 5 F1
Ridgeway Special School
  WWCK CV34 .... 2 D1
Rother House Medical Centre
  STRAT CV37 .... 6 C3
Royal Leamington Spa
  Rehabilitation Hospital
  WWCK CV34 .... 23 E1
Royal Shakespeare Theatre
  STRAT CV37 .... 7 F5
Royal Shakespeare
  Theatre Workshop
  STRAT CV37 .... 27 E2
St Anthonys RC Primary School
  RLSS CV31 .... 5 K5
St Anthonys RC Primary School
  RLSS CV31 .... 19 E3
St Gregors Primary School
  STRAT CV37 .... 7 F2
St John's House Museum
  WWCK CV34 .... 2 C5